PLEASING THE LORD

Knowing God's Will and Receiving His Rewards

by

Norvel Hayes

NORVEL HAYES MINISTRIES

"... and he gave them power and authority over all
devils and to cure diseases."

Unless otherwise indicated, all Scripture quotations are taken from the *King James Version* of the Bible.

Pleasing the Lord
Knowing God's Will and Receiving His Rewards
ISBN 1-57794-033-4
Copyright © 1997 by Norvel Hayes
P. O. Box 1379
Cleveland, Tennessee 37311

Published by Norvel Hayes Ministries
P.O. Box 1379
Cleveland, TN 37364-1379

Contents

• • •

Introduction
• • •

Pleasing the Lord is simple. But many people don't understand how simple it really is. First Timothy 4:1 says, **the Spirit expressly says that in the latter times some shall depart from the faith, giving heed to seducing spirits, and doctrines of devils.** The devil has separated some of our brothers and sisters who once knew and walked in the power of the world of God's "unseen" faith.

Some have departed from the faith after working for God a while, thinking they can please the Lord by saying or doing just any old thing.

Others have departed from the faith by seducing spirits that have goofed up their thinking and have been led over into the devil's world of natural reasoning.

But, glory to God, there are many others who have continued to please the Lord by obeying Him. They live in God's *right now* world of unseen faith.

Book of Hebrews faith is *right now* faith, because:

> *Now faith* **is the substance of things hoped for, the evidence of things not seen.**
>
> **Hebrews 11:6**

Right now faith always worships the Lord and says and believes what God wants to do — *right now!* It doesn't reason about this, or that, or why, or why not.

I wrote this book to teach and remind us of the Lord Jesus' blessed faith commandments. Because doing what the Word says like the Lord Jesus taught in the Gospels always pleases Him. And those who want to please the Lord always get blessed. Always!

Two Worlds:
Faith and Unbelief
• • •

Several years ago a chiropractor in Harrisburg, Pennsylvania, invited me to speak at a Full Gospel Businessmen's Banquet on a Saturday night and at his church on Sunday morning. Harrisburg is kind of in the bottom part of the state, and I was scheduled to speak in Williamsport Sunday evening. So he called me on the phone and asked if I could stop in. He said they were doing the work of God and needed some help, so I told him I would be glad to do it.

We left on Sunday afternoon, and got there around three o'clock. The banquet hall was full of Pentecostal pastors and leaders from that city. I mean I had to actually work my way around to even get a place to stand up. They had a big banquet spread with all kinds of good food and asked if I would like to eat before answering questions. But I told them to go ahead with the ministry session first.

The place was so packed I had to actually push myself through the crowd to get up to the platform. Looking the crowd over, I greeted them and asked for the first question.

Then a nice looking fellow stood up and said, "Brother Norvel, I belong to a local church here in town, and my wife and I have a ministry downtown where we work with dope addicts in a coffee house type of thing. We're not rebels of the church. I'm in agreement with my pastor, and he approves of our ministry. We work together and pray for people all the time and see them set free from dope." Then he said, "We're Full Gospel Pentecostal people, but I have to ask you a question. Ah, I have a disease in my body, an affliction, and my wife has one, and we prayed and prayed, and other people have prayed. And I want to ask you, Brother Norvel, why doesn't God heal us?"

The moment he said that to me, the Holy Spirit on the inside of me went bssssssshhh! He shot a verse of Scripture in my mind, and said to me just as quick as you could bat your eye, "Flag him down; he's on the wrong road. Tell him the verse."

Before I answered his question, I told the group, "Many of you won't understand this, but you will in a few minutes." Then I turned to the man, and said, "Mister, Jesus won't heal you because you've been committing sin."

Well, I might as well have hit him in the face with a wet dishrag. He went, "Ah — ah!" and said, "No. No, Brother Norvel, I — I — I haven't been committing any sin — I live my life right. I'm not involved in any sin."

So I said, "Well, let me ask you a question. Do you understand English?"

He said, "Well, yes."

Then I said, "Jesus won't heal you because you've been committing sin. Is that clear?"

He said, "Ah — ah, I — I don't know what to say...really, Brother Norvel, I haven't been committing any sin. I'm living my life right. At least I haven't committed any sin."

Then he turned to his wife to check up on her and said, "We live our life right, don't we, Honey? Have we? uh, er, Honey; have you?"

But she was just as dumbfounded as he was and said, "No, I haven't committed any sin."

So I said, "Well, both of you need to look at me now." And they both stared at me as I said, "Listen closely. Jesus will not heal you because you've been committing sin. Is that clear?"

I could tell he was having a hard time with my answer, but I wanted to make a point. Because if God doesn't answer your prayers, there's always a reason why. Healing has already been paid for, yet, they weren't getting healed. And I wanted to teach, not only him, but the whole group what can hinder the promises of God.

So I looked at the man and asked him again, "Where have you been committing sin?" Then I answered my own question, "I'll tell you where you're in sin. You're a doubter, and you've left the world of faith. And even though you have a ministry, and you're in good standing with your pastor and your church, you've left the world of faith and have gotten over into the sin of unbelief."

"Oh really?" he asked. "What's the verse of Scripture the Holy Ghost gave you? Where is that in the Bible?"

WHATSOEVER IS NOT OF FAITH IS SIN
• • •

So I told him to turn to Romans 14:23 and I read, **...for whatsoever is not of faith is sin.**

Then I turned to the crowd and said, "Many of you people here this afternoon are wanting your healing, too.

You want it very much, but until you understand this truth, you're not going to get it. There's no use in just wandering around and thinking, *Maybe, God in His goodness will help me someday.* 'Someday' may be too late. God wants you to have faith in Him *right now.* Because *Now faith is the substance.*"

Then I looked at the man again and said, "Now listen closely," and I quoted 1 Timothy 4:1: **Now the Spirit speaketh expressly, that in the latter times some shall depart from the faith, giving heed to seducing spirits, and doctrines of devils.**"

"The devil has seducing spirits," I went on. "And if you want to know the truth about it, the devil has seducing spirits that get hold of your mind. They'll cause you to think in a certain realm or area of your life to go down a certain avenue, and that avenue will seem right. But it's outside the book of faith, the Book of Hebrews. And when you step out of God's world of faith, and start in the world of reasoning, you have just left God."

"God doesn't honor the world of reasoning or making excuses for faith," I continued. "Now, there is safety in reasoning things out among each other if you have someone who knows what they're doing. But there's no use trying to reason things out with a bunch of Bible-ignorant dummies. That's not going to help you at all."

Then I said, "If you want to know why the Lord's not doing something for you, always have a dedicated faith teacher present before you ever start reasoning it out. Because if you start reasoning something out with people that think like you, they'll just make excuses. They'll say things like, 'Well, uh, you're a good person,' and this and that. And, 'The Lord won't look on this as sin...you know, God has His own timing....'" And they will go on with, God has this, and God has that, but the time for you to believe the Bible is right now! Faith is right now! And it takes faith to please the Lord — Bible faith that does everything *you do* to please the Lord.

Finally, I told this group, "Many of you people in here are wanting your healing real bad. You'd like to have your healing, and you want it real bad, but until you change, you're not going to get your healing. You can't doubt God and get out the world of continually giving thanks and speaking God's Word and get Him to heal you, because He doesn't approve of doubt. *He hates doubt!* Get that straight! All of it! He hates it. And *wondering* is just as bad as doubt. *Wondering, wondering, wondering.* You don't have to wonder. All you have to do is take God at His Word, and healing is yours now!"

Well, I can tell you that I didn't leave that group *wondering* that afternoon.

RIGHT NOW FAITH!
. . .

How can you please the Lord? First of all, my brother, make up your mind that you will believe God by faith **right now!** Always remember this, my sister: someday with God never comes. The only thing God ever approves of in your believing is faith in Him RIGHT NOW!

So don't wait. Sometimes we judge ourselves and think we're good Christians because we go to church. We do this and that, and because God blesses us with His love, we can receive a love blessing. But God will bless you with a love blessing today and let you die next week. Get that straight! Healing my brother, just like finances and all of God's blessings, is a benefit of the believer. But, my sister, you have to please Him to receive it. And you please the Lord with faith. God loves you whether you get healed or not. But He *wants* to heal you now with RIGHT NOW faith! He wants to bless you with His presence and joy now, with RIGHT NOW faith! He wants to bless you with finances now, with RIGHT NOW faith!

Right Talk Pleasing Faith

• • •

The beautiful part about God is, He will do anything He says He will do. And the beautiful part about the Gospel is, He will do it for you! That is, if you say it. Glory to God forever! He does it for *me,* and He will do it for *you.*

Some time back a nationally known evangelist along with some other Full Gospel evangelists came to me wanting to talk in private. They asked me the same thing the man in Harrisburg did, "Brother Norvel, we see the Lord heal people all the time through our hands, but we all have infirmities, why doesn't He heal us?"

So I told them why, "Because you don't talk right. There's a calling upon your lives, an anointing, and it's been given to you to bring healing to others. But you've left the world of faith for yourselves."

"What do you mean 'we don't talk right?'" they asked.

So I answered, "Do you ever walk the floor and call Jesus your own personal Healer? Do you ever walk the floor and say, "Jesus, I believe that You are the Healer. I see You heal people every night through me. Now Lord, I also believe You are my own personal Healer"?

13

If you want the Lord to heal you, you have to make Him your own personal Healer, just like you made Him your personal Savior. You have to come to a place that your mouth will speak words of victory up to heaven that say, "Jesus, you are my personal Healer. Jesus, "YOU ARE MY PERSONAL HEALER AND YOU ARE HEALING ME NOW!"

If you want to please God *big* for your healing, say, "God by Your stripes I am healed and Your healing power is welcome in my body. Your healing power is flowing through me to heal and set me free. Thank You, Lord, for driving all affliction out of my body. I will not put up with affliction or disease, in Jesus' name."

If your right leg is infirm, say, "I take authority over this weakness, and I command all weakness to leave my right leg. Jesus, You are my own personal Healer, and I believe that Your healing power is flowing through my right leg now to drive out all weakness and disease, and give me strength, in Jesus' name."

And you can do the same for any other affliction or disease.

THE LORD DOES WHAT YOU SAY AND DO
• • •

The Lord does what you say. And the Lord does what you do. He is everything. Jesus is, Alpha, and Omega, the beginning, and the ending of your life. He is everything!

The Lord Jesus Christ is the Savior; He is the Healer; He is the Deliverer; He is the Miracle Worker. He is the Financial Blesser. But He will never be that to you until you call Him that.

You have to come to the place where you no longer have to ask, "Why won't God heal me?"

Do you read your Bible? It says your healing is already paid for. Jesus is the Healer. All through the Bible He tells you that. He revealed Himself as Healer long before He showed Himself as Savior:

> **I am the Lord that healeth thee.**
>
> **Exodus 15:26**

If you want God to work for you — if you want God's mighty power to help you — you have to come to a place where you get over into the world of faith and the Word. Quote the Word, talk victory all the time. Faith has a voice of victory, not a voice of doubt.

Never open up your mouth and start wondering, "Well, I don't know why God won't heal me...or, maybe it's not God's will to heal me...."

Stop that stuff. Don't do that anymore. If you've been talking like that, stop it today. If you don't, the devil will have so many doors open in your life that he will just come in and start putting things on you. You have a divine right to stop him in Jesus' name.

No Respecter of Persons
· · ·

Because I walk in God's blessings, do I think God loves me more than He loves you? NO! There's no such thing as that. Do you think He blesses me financially and keeps me healthy and does all these wonderful things for me because I am in the ministry? Or because I have a home for unwed mothers? Or because I have a ministry to abused children and a Bible school, and because I teach and preach all over the world?

The answer to all of that is, NO, He doesn't. If you want to know the truth about it, I get nothing from God unless I claim it. I talk right. And I take time every morning to worship Him...just worship the Lord first thing...and praise Him, and tell Him my life belongs to Him. I say, "I want to please You, God, I want to please You, Lord, I want to please You." And when I do that, I read my Bible and pray and tell Him I believe Him by faith. Then my heart stays a heart of flesh instead of a heart of stone.

I don't want my heart to turn to a heart of stone, and become Gospel hardened. I sometimes meet Gospel evangelists and Gospel preachers, and I feel so sorry for them. It's like their minds have been seared over with the Gospel. They call it "Gospel hardened, but it's not really the Gospel that's hardened them. It's more like *burn out*, and I feel so sorry for them.

THE HUMBLE PLEASE GOD
. . .

A man with a humble and hungry heart finds great favor with God. When you bow down before God, and show Him that you mean business, and worship Him, and praise Him, God just loves that. He loves to see you worshipping and praising Him. He just loves to see you walking the floor, and hearing you confess that He is God. He loves to hear you confess, "By the stripes of Jesus, the Son of God, I am healed. Oh, God, by the stripes of Jesus I am healed. Lord, by the stripes of Jesus I am healed. Health belongs to me!"

I talk to the Lord like He is my best friend. And I tell the Lord I want to stay out of this sin business. I tell Him I know that He hates doubt — and that unless I believe Him by faith — unless I believe those stripes on Jesus' back were for my healing — I know that I will miss out on my healing and I will be slaughtered by some disease, unless I eat from His table daily.

The only reason our squirrely minds begin to wonder about why God does or doesn't do this or that is because we haven't been eating the Book of Hebrews. When is the last time that you quoted from Hebrews 11:6: **Without faith it is impossible to please him?**

Did you know that you can give money to God, and you can sing songs to God, and you can pray and pray until your jaws get sore. You can speak in tongues until you have to rest your mouth. You can do all of this, but without faith it is impossible to please the Lord?

"Whoa...wait a minute," you say, "that man in Pennsylvania told you he loved the Lord."

That's right. But my message to him out of Romans 14:23 was that he was in sin for being separated from Jesus *the Healer*. Not Jesus *the Lover*. Or Jesus *the Savior*. Or Jesus *the Blesser*. He was separated by his intellect and his doubting. So his body was separated from God's healing power because he allowed doubt to come in, **for whatever is not of faith is sin** (Romans 14:23). And sin separates from the blessing of God.

17

YOU CAN'T SAY JUST ANYTHING YOU WANT
AND PLEASE THE LORD
• • •

Sometimes we get so religious in working for God that we think we can do or say anything we want to because we are working for God. We think, *Well, He will heal me because I minister the Full Gospel message.*

No He won't! He won't heal you dear Full Gospel leader, because He said if you doubt Him, you're in sin. That type of a sin separates healing from you. It doesn't separate you from a relationship with God — it separates you from healing. Then it causes your mind to go into a world of wondering, *Why doesn't God heal me? I'm a Full Gospel leader. I love the Lord, why doesn't He heal me?*

I have heard Brother Kenneth Hagin, Sr. say, "I haven't had a headache in fifty-two years...I've had several real bad headaches to hit me, but they never did last over a minute. Because the minute that stinging pain hit me, I said, 'No you don't. No you don't.'"

MAKE THE DEVIL NERVOUS
• • •

So the greatest word you will ever say to the devil in your life has two little letters. The greatest word that you will ever say in your life to any kind of the works of hell is "No! Nooooo you don't; not to me." "Nooooo sin!" "Nooooo disease!" "Nooooo sadness!" "Nooooo!" "Nooooo!"

When the devil comes and tries to tempt you in any way, or put a disease on you, or a pain or any of his wiles, all you say is, "No! No! No, I WON'T ACCEPT THAT!"

If tomorrow the pain is worse, you need to continue to say, "NOOOUUU. NOOOOO, I won't accept that." Then if on the third day the pain is worse, stand up again and say, "NOOOOOOO!"

The devil is hard of hearing. So when the pain gets worse, you get louder and longer. It makes the devil nervous. And after a few days you will get so loud and so long with your resisting and your NOOOOOOOOO, that he goes, "OWWWWWWWWWW!" and leaves. He does. I'm not kidding you — it's the truth.

Now I am going to say something that may sound mean to you, but I am going to tell you the truth. If you are sick today, the only reason why is that you didn't say "NO" to the devil. No you didn't. You didn't press on through doubt, fear, discouragement, and demonic harassment. You didn't bind the devil and keep binding him. But you can, because Jesus said, **I give you power over all the enemy, and nothing shall by any means hurt you** (Luke 10:19, author's paraphrase). We are in a war. We can't just sit in our living room chair and be nice and say, "You shouldn't do this to me, Satan." Are you kidding? The devil eats words like that for lunch.

You need to learn to tell the devil to eat your NO'S — "NOOOOOOOOOOOOOOO, I WON'T RECEIVE THIS! I won't accept it, and I bind you, devil, and all your little demons, in the name of Jesus Christ Who said I could!" Then begin to praise the Lord Jesus Christ as your personal Healer and Deliverer.

God said it first:

> **I am the Lord that healeth thee.**
>
> **Exodus 15:26**

19

Holy Ghost Prayer Pleasing Faith

...before him whom he believed, even God,
who quickeneth the dead, and calleth those things
which be not as though they were.

Romans 4:17

Now I want to get real with you. I want to tell you
how the devil came against my finances and afflicted my
daughter physcially, and how talking faith's talk became
real to me.

In the early days of my ministry I didn't know the
importance of the offices of the church. The only thing I
really knew was, I was a successful businessman making
five or six thousand dollars a week, and everything I had
was paid for, plus my four Cadillacs. But one day, I realized
that everything I earned, and everything I had, didn't satisfy
me. In fact, I was miserable and I didn't know what was
wrong. It was so bad that I came to a point that there was
no one else to turn to, and I gave my life to God.

At that point in my life, I had never heard of Kenneth
Hagin, Sr., but the Holy Ghost spoke sovereignly to each
of us, thousands of miles apart, and put us together in a
way that only He can.

Brother Hagin was in California conducting a meeting when a word from the Lord came to him saying, "Go to Washington, D.C., for the Full Gospel Businessmen's Convention. You are going to meet a man that you are divinely destined to meet."

Little did I know that I was that man. I was in Tennessee carrying on my businesses when one day the Holy Spirit pulled me up into the Spirit world and showed me Brother Hagin. I knew I was supposed to bring Brother Hagin to Tennessee for a meeting. This was some twenty years ago.

So, God sent me to Washington, D.C., to attend the Full Gospel Businessmen's Convention. And when I saw Brother Hagin, I walked up to him and I said, "Brother Hagin, the Lord pulled me up into His presence and told me that He wants you to come to Cleveland, Tennessee."

Brother Hagin said, "I know it; I know it. I'll come. I'll come. I saw you."

And I thought, *Oh, my God! What kind of a human being is this? I'm just a businessman trying to find a building; I don't know anything about God to speak of....*

THANK GOD FOR THE OFFICE OF THE PROPHET!

• • •

Later, I found out how *dangerous* it is to go to a Kenneth Hagin service. Especially when a man walks in the office of the prophet. But it can also be one of the greatest blessings in the world. Thank God for the office of the prophet! The offices of the church are so wonderful. And I sense in my spirit that the Body of Christ is hungry for the ministry of the church offices.

I am not a prophet, I am a teacher. God just unfolds the Bible to me and tells me to teach it. Today I teach it everywhere. But Brother Hagin walks in the office of the prophet. And that night in Washington D.C., I was sitting in the congregation where he was teaching, when all of a sudden, the Spirit of God came up on him, and he began to prophesy.

In the prophecy, he called my name, and said, "Norvel Hayes, the devil is going to attack your finances, but if you will pray, and pray, and pray, and pray, you will come through the attack. 'But you must be faithful to Me, and you must pray, and pray, and pray, and when you have come through the attack, it will change your life. When you come through the attack, you will be more successful, financially, than you've ever been.'"

Well, I thought, *What does he mean by that?*

I had never had any trouble, financially. Then, about six months went by. Brother Hagin was somewhere preaching, and at that particular time in my life I was down in Florida. I had bought a two hundred acre subdivision on which I developed 544 lots and built five miles of streets, paying cash for all of it as I went. I also owned six restaurants as side investments, my own ring manufacturing company, and just a bunch of stuff. Then about six months after that prophecy, the devil hit my businesses. And did he ever — he really attacked me. I'm telling you, it was something else.

One of my restaurant managers went bad. And then another one went bad. And then another one went bad. Then the Holy Ghost said to me one night, "Go to Columbus, Ohio, where your manufacturing company is, and check your books."

Well, I knew there was something wrong, or He would not have told me to do that. So I took a man who was knowledgeable with me and we went out to the manufacturing company about eleven or twelve o'clock one night. We went in and checked the books, and found that one of the employees — the secretary, had stolen thousands and thousands of dollars. So much money had been stolen, that I was going to have to sell the plant.

The next morning, I went to my corporation lawyer's office and laid all the information on his desk. He gave it a quick look and said, "Norvel, this is a state corporation, and you don't have to press any charges. All you have to do is take this material to the District Attorney's office and they'll do everything else. It'll be the state of Ohio versus her. And I can tell you right now that she'll go to the penitentiary for three years. But for good behavior, she could get out in a year-and-a-half or two years. But she will definitely get three years for embezzlement of a state corporation."

I said, "Well, she's been working for me for years, and before this, she was a good employee. I don't want to see her go to jail."

"Well, Norvell," the lawyer told me, "you're going to have to make up your mind concerning what you want to do: either take the loss, or she'll go to the penitentiary."

So I decided to take the loss and sold the manufacturing company.

Remember, the Holy Ghost had told me, through Brother Hagin's prophecy, "...the devil is going to attack your finances."

Thank God for the office of the prophet! The Holy Ghost can operate through him, or any Spirit-filled person, to tell you what the devil's going to do in the future. Glory to God forever.

In the middle of all of this, I was trying to pray, but all of my businesses were gone, except for one little restaurant. Month after month, it was all out-go and no income. I couldn't sell one lot in my subdivision down in Florida. The manager of every restaurant I had went flaky. And my good help that had been with me for years, was stealing money from me.

GOOD SENSE
• • •

So I had lost all my restaurants, my manufacturing plant, and now my daughter, Zona, was afflicted with boils all over her body. That's right, boils! The devil put boils all over my daughter's body. I didn't know what to do, so I just kept on doing the work of God. I wasn't making very much profit, but I would take what little profit I did make, and I would go buy groceries for the poor. In the midst of it all, I just kept on passing out tracts and praying. I just *acted* like I had good sense.

During this time, one of the best known candy companies in America would give us a pickup truck load of candy whenever we wanted it. We would sack it up in little sacks, and give it to poor kids. Then, we would take them to church on Sunday. A big rental van company would give crushed ice flavored "snowballs" to the little poor kids on Saturdays. On top of the sack of snowballs, we would give them a little Bible, all free.

We would go to their neighborhoods and talk to the parents and ask them to come to church. At the beginning of our children's ministry, we had one school bus. But after about three or four years of that, we had eight, all full of little kids. Finally, we had so many kids in church, we had to build another church. We built another sanctuary and called it "Little People's Church." Glory to God!

Then, we hired a youth pastor and he would preach to the kids every Sunday while the main pastor was preaching to the adults.

I just kept on working, like I had good sense, calling myself successful: "I'm successful in Jesus' name." But my mind would say, *are you kidding me? You're everything but successful.* So I would walk the floor and say, "I am successful in Jesus' name. I have a right to **confess things that be not as though they were**" (Romans 4:17, author's paraphrase).

I tell you, it's hell to own a bunch of businesses, and not make any profits. There were times when I wished someone else owned every business I had. It was like a curse.

Things got so bad that I went to work for Sears and Roebuck making $150 a week. It was better than trying to run deadbeat businesses. Who on God's green earth wants to own a bunch of businesses if they're not making profits?

The devil had attacked my businesses, and he had put forty-two knots and growths all over my daughter's body, I mean — dear God in heaven. But I said, "I have a right to **call those things that be not thought they were**" (Romans 4:17).

I knew Jesus said, Not that which goeth into the mouth defileth a man; but that which cometh out of the mouth, this defileth a man (Matthew 15:11). And that it was what comes out of my mouth that defiles me. I knew words that I spoke out of my mouth could defile me or put me over. So I watched my mouth. I wouldn't go through any pity parties, and I watched my dedication to God.

Every day I would bind up every work of hell that attacked my businesses, and say, "I command you, Satan, take your hand off of my businesses! I call myself successful! I call myself successful. I call myself successful. I call myself successful!"

I was being attacked fiancially and then the devil began to put boils and knots and growths all over my daughter's body. There wasn't a single person in my family I could turn to, because no one, not one of my family, was serving the Lord. Talk about Job! My daughter Zona had boils and knots and growths all over her body, and I was being attacked in my businesses.

At that time I didn't have any problem praying for my businesses, but I didn't know a whole lot about healing. I had learned a little from Brother Hagin, and others. Still, I had never really tried to pray for anyone's healing. But desperate people do desperate things, and I was beginning to get desperate. Anyone or anything that touched my daughter had me to deal with!

I began, "Oh, Lord, I pray that You would heal my daughter. Oh, God, I pray that Your healing power will come upon my daughter and remove those growths, and all those knots, and all of those awful looking things off her body. Oh, God, remove them off of her. Remove them off of her. Remove them off of her, in Jesus' name!" Then I would pray and praise, and pray, and praise, and pray, and praise. If you want to know the truth about it, I was about to wear myself out praying and praising for both Zona and my businesses.

This went on for about two or three years. That's right! Two or three years! Faith has patience. Faith has patience all the time! Because, **The trying of your faith worketh patience** (James 1:3).

Well, after I had been speaking and binding up the work of hell for all that time, I asked my personal secretary, who has been with me for more than twenty years, and is very efficient, "Mary Lou, how much money do I have in the bank after I pay you Friday?"

She said, "You have eighty-five dollars."

So I said, "Eighty-five dollars to run all these businesses?"

"That's what you have," she said.

I thought, *If an air conditioner would break down in one of these buildings, it might cost five or six thousand to get it fixed.* That's how the devil messes with your mind.

But it was then that I said, "Eighty-five dollars? Mary Lou, I don't accept that. I see thousands and thousands and thousands of dollars in there, don't you?"

She said, "Whatever you say, Mr. Hayes."

"That's what I say," I told her. "Faith is not seen, and I have every right to call those things that be not as though they were. I said I see thousands of dollars in there, don't you, Mary Lou?"

She said, "Whatever you say."

And I said, "Well, that's what I say."

"Good," she said.

Well praise the Lord! I was just being bold enough to call those things that be not of as though they were (Romans 4:17). I was calling myself successful. For three years, I called myself successful, and my daughter healed.

So now you ask, "Norvel, did she get healed then? And did your businesses begin to make a profit?"

No. In fact, they got worse.

So, what did I do?

LIKEWISE THE SPIRIT...
• • •

I just kept on like I had good sense, calling myself successful, and calling my daughter healed. "Oh, God, I ask You, Lord, to heal my daughter, and bless my businesses."

Then one day I went home and I learned a good lesson on this. I was reading in my Bible, and suddenly words jumped out at me from the page. I found that the Bible said, **if I would let the Holy Ghost pray, instead of me praying in my natural mind, I could have anything I wanted** (Romans 8:26, author's paraphrase).

Then I said out loud, "What? What? Yeah! Have anything you want." And I said, "Is that right?" and I read it again:

> Likewise the Spirit also helpeth our infirmities: for we know not what we should pray for as we ought: but the Spirit itself maketh intercession for us with groanings which cannot be uttered.
>
> And he that searcheth the hearts knoweth what is the mind of the Spirit, because he maketh intercession for the saints according to the will of God.
>
> **Romans 8:26,27**

The will of God *is victory* in everything about your life. There is no defeat in God.

You ask, "Well, how do you know it's the will of God?"

So I say, "Show me in the Bible where defeat is the will of God."

Being broke, and sick is not the will of God. An afflicted body is not the will of God. Do you want me to say, "Well, if the Lord wants my daughter to keep knots and growths all over her, the rest of her life, I'll just glorify the Lord"? That's ignorance gone to seed.

IT'S UP TO YOU
• • •

When you think defeat in any area of your life, you're not accepting the Lord Jesus Christ as a Healer. You're not accepting Him as a Miracle Worker. You have a right to have healing, and you have a right to have a miracle, and so do your children. But it's up to you to take it away from the devil.

Proven, Tested, Pleasing Faith
. . .

Once I learned the great secret of Romans 8:26,27 that showed me I could pray in tongues while the Holy Spirit would take what I said in the Spirit, straighten it out, and give it to God, I started mixing my confession in English and tongues! I would go into my office at nighttime, and would pray in tongues for a while, then I would pray in English. I would pray, "I call myself successful. I call myself successful." Then I would pray in tongues, "I call my daughter healed." Then I would pray in English, then in tongues. And I would pray that way for hours.

I did that for several months. Then, finally, I went down to my home office, looked at the "big company checkbook," you know, big deal, "eighty-five dollars" — I would open up my checkbook, to see the balance. Then I would lay it open on top of the desk and pray in tongues. Then I would pray in English, then in tongues, then in English. I would call myself successful. I would say, "In Jesus' name, I see thousands and thousands of dollars in my checkbook. In Jesus' name, I call thousands of dollars in there." Then I would laugh in the Spirit.

You ask, "Were you full of joy?"

No, I just acted like I was. I made myself do it. Sometimes you have to make yourself do it, because ...**the joy of the Lord is your strength** (Nehemiah 8:10b).

FAITH DOESN'T WEAR A WATCH
• • •

After a few weeks of that, I would get louder, and sometimes my laughing in the Spirit would get weaker. But I always did it. Always! Always! I would say, "The joy of the Lord is my strength!" And I would say it over and over and over and over.

Faith doesn't wear a watch. And if you ever get *time* mixed up with faith, you will jump out of the Book of Hebrews and be out on your own.

"But Brother Norvel, when do you think the manfestation will come?"

Now listen closely: If you get time involved with faith, you will bog the manifestation down, and it will take it ten times as long to come. Ten times! Or it may never come. There's no wondering about faith in God. Leave time to God. No wondering, just faith.

NO PITY PARTIES
• • •

I just kept on working for God, helping little poor kids and stinking people while my daughter was covered with boils and my business was under attack, with no pity parties. I would go down to my office and lay my checkbook open, and I would pray in tongues. Then I would pray in English, "I am successful in Jesus' name, I call my daughter healed in Jesus' name, I am successful in

Jesus' name." I started getting happy about it. "By the eye of faith I'm successful in Jesus' name, I see thousands and thousands of dollars in Jesus' name!"

Then I would go home to my daughter. She was the only family I had, because all the rest of the family had left me because I was serving the Lord in the Full Gospel Movement. A "proper" kind of religion would have been all right, but they didn't want to get involved in "that kind of stuff."

My daughter was covered with boils, and knots, and growths, and my businesses were gone. Sometimes I felt like I was Job, Jr. But I still had my Bible and the Holy Ghost lived in me. And I was still working for God, I still had the victory, and I was still praying in tongues.

Then one day after I had just finished a meeting in San Antonio, I was sitting alone in my motel room waiting for some missionaries to take me to the airport. I was fixing to catch a plane to go to Chattanooga. But the Spirit of God moved upon me and overshadowed me and said, "Don't go home. Go to Tulsa, Oklahoma, and I'll show you two things after you get there...."

Always remember this: When you're going through a trial, God will see you through, and you will receive the manifestation of your prayers, if you can pass the final test.

The plane touched down in Oklahoma City, and I called Brother Kenneth Hagin and said, "Brother Hagin, the Lord told me to come to Tulsa. He said He would show me two things after I got here."

Brother Hagin said, "Come on over. We've stayed in your house a lot of times, come and have dinner with us."

I said, "No." But he insisted, so I agreed. At that particular time I knew only three people in Tulsa, Oklahoma. I knew Brother Hagin, Oral Roberts, and a man named Ford, who had helped Demas Shakarian start the Full Gospel Businessmen's Fellowship.

About the second day after I arrived in Tulsa, I was sitting in Brother Hagin's house when all of a sudden, a spirit of intercession came upon me. Oretha Hagin, Kenneth Hagin's wife, heard me, and came in and said, "Brother Norvel, do you want us to pray with you?" I said, "Yes."

They had other guests at the time, so she called them and Brother Hagin over.

Then we got on our knees, all around the fireplace, and we began to pray. After we prayed a while, I got up and began to walk the floor. I began walking back and forth and praying, back and forth, back and forth. Then, now listen to this, somebody wanted me to pray for *them,* and while I was praying, Brother Hagin got up and left the room. As I continued to groan in the Spirit, and cry out to the Lord, the Lord said, "You can go home now. I brought you here to pray for *that* person, so you can go now."

Brother Hagin had gone to the back room to continue praying where he was groaning and praying in the Spirit. When he finished, I said, "Brother Hagin, the Lord told me I can go home now."

"He did?"

"Yes."

Then Brother Hagin asked if I could stay a few more days.

I thanked him, but said I had to go, and asked if he could drive me to the airport. So he took me to the airport.

Now on the way to the airport (you aren't going to believe this, glory to God).... On the way to the airport with this same man who years earlier prophesied how the devil was going to attack my businesses and finances, said, "Brother Norvel, the Lord moved on me this morning back there in my prayer room. He said to tell you that you've passed His test, and the light of God is going to shine down from heaven, down upon your finances, and never again, as long as you live, will you ever have any want."

By then, I wasn't sure I needed a plane to fly home. Glory be to God!

About two weeks went by, and a real estate company called me on the phone and a man said, "Mr. Hayes, I have a buyer for that little piece of property you have listed with us. I see you paid $13,000.00, but my buyer will give you $28,000.00 for it. Would you be willing to sell it?"

Real calm, I said, "Yeah, I think so. I believe I'll sell that."

Another week went by, and the same real estate man called me again, and said, "Mr. Hayes, that piece of property that you own on the country road — I don't know if you know it or not, but the county has come by, and paved that dirt road in front of it. I know what you paid for it, and you can get almost three times what you gave for it. Would you be willing to sell it?"

So I said, "Why not? As you know, I only gave $1,500.00 for it."

Not long after selling those two properties, I made another transaction for property that I had given $55,000.00

for and sold it for nearly half a million! Then I asked, "Lord, what am I going to do with all this money?"

He said, "You're going to spend it for me, or I am going to take it away from you."

Thank You, Lord.

Obedient Faith
(The Day I Didn't Go Fishing)
• • •

Not long after God began to turn my finances around, my close friend, Vep Ellis, (the man who wrote so many great Gospel songs) and I were riding up Highway 19 north from St. Petersburg, Florida. Vep and I were going fishing with one of his deacons. It was just about daylight, and I was following them in my car. But there was so much fog, I got lost from them. For a minute, I got real worried. Then, suddenly, the Holy Ghost came upon me and said, "Don't go fishing today. I want you to buy a piece of property for Me, and I want you to use this property to win some of these elderly people in Florida to Me."

He continued, "Son, buy this piece of property for Me and begin to train mission workers to reach every one in this area. I want you to send them out, two by two, from house to house. And I want you to work these towns and villages all around here." He specified a certain section, and said, "Just knock on doors, and leave a tract. That's all I want you to do."

Then the Spirit said, "Don't invite any one to come and hold a meeting, just knock on the doors of individual homes. These are Jewish and Italian people who used to live in New York City. And there are many people from Pittsburgh, Baltimore, Philadelphia, and other places — they live in a totally different world. They will live the last days of their lives here. They will play golf as long as they are able, shuffleboard, have their parties, and just live out their lives and wait to die. But I want you to bring some of them to heaven, and give them a little heaven to go to heaven in."

Then He showed me five little bitty acres of property with a dirty looking motel on it, and I bought it. It cost me $90,000.00.

Then, I began to send out workers door-to-door, trailer-to-trailer, apartment-to-apartment, and condo-to-condo. I said, "Don't miss a trailer. Understand me, workers, don't miss a trailer. If there's no one at home, leave a tract. Leave salvation tracts and healing tracts. Don't miss a door in this town. Go street-by-street, and trailer court-by-trailer court. Don't miss a living soul. I don't care if it's a five million dollar mansion or an old rusty trailer that's not worth a thousand dollars. Make sure the Gospel gets into that home, and into the hands of the people."

In obedience to the Lord, I would send people out two-by-two in ten or twelve cars, armed with thousands of tracts. That was more than ten years ago. Then one day, a real estate man called me and said, "I know you paid $90,000 for that piece of property ten years ago, but I have a buyer who wants to give you $1,400,000.00 for it."

"You mean, I could make over a million dollars cash for it right now?" I asked.

"Right now," he said. "So, you do want to sell, don't you?"

But I told him, "Are you kidding? What do I want a million dollars for? I deal in souls. If I did sell it, I'd build something else just like it, or even better."

I built a sanctuary on that million dollar property, and now we have preaching, teaching, and healing meetings, and whatever else the Lord directs. That's what happens to you when you put the Gospel first, my brother. Put the Gospel first. You could be a millionaire by just obeying the Holy Ghost *one* time.

ZONA HEALED!
. . .

Then one day when I was praying for my daughter's healing, Zona's manifestation happened. By now, Zona had places on her hand that were split and bleeding, and knots and growths all were over her legs and knees, forty-two of them. And the Lord said, "Son, you are not declaring right; you are declaring wrong. Stop praying, 'Lord, would You heal my daughter?' and curse those things on your daughter's body. Curse those knots and boils. Curse the very root of them in My name, and they will die and disappear. Then after you curse them, call her free from boils. Call your daughter free from those knots and growths, and thank Me for removing them."

So I cursed them in Jesus' name and said, "I curse the roots of you knots and growths! I command you to die and fall off of my daughter's body in Jesus' name." I said, "Leave her! Leave her in Jesus' name!" and I walked the floor doing it for about forty days.

"Thank You, Lord, I call Zona free from growths and knots! I call Zona free in Jesus' name. Thank You, Lord, for Your healing power coming, and overshadowing her, and removing all the growths off of her."

One afternoon, after about forty days of thanking and praising God, and calling those things that be not as though they were, Zona was hanging up some of her dresses. It was about 5 PM. She had taken all of her dresses out of her closet, and laid them on the bed to sort them out — winter from summer. And while she was in the middle of hanging up her dresses like this, just minding her own business, you know, she started to turn around to get another dress...and,...she goes, "AWWWWWWWOW!" She saw herself in the mirror and every growth on her body had disappeared. And new skin came all over her. Glory to God forever!

Today Zona often looks up at me with tears in her eyes and says, "Daddy, had it not been for your faith, I would have knots and growths all over me and probably be in hell now. But, your faith in God for me has made me whole."

Glory to God for His healing power for those who will walk the floor and curse the works of darkness and receive His healing gifts!

GIVING THANKS PLEASES GOD
· · ·

> In every thing give thanks: for this is the will
> of God in Christ Jesus concerning you.
> 1 Thessalonians 5:18

Later the Lord instructed me, "Tell My children not to forget to thank Me for everything. Because if they forget to thank Me for everything, I forget to give it to them. I have it set up that way. Tell them to remind Me of what I have promised them (Isaiah 43:26). Tell them I have it set up that way, and that I want them to remind me of the Scripture they are claiming. Tell them to give thanks for the Scripture they are believing. And tell them that when they speak My Word, it gets My attention."

Worship Pleasing Faith
. . .

Then Jesus went thence, and departed into the
coasts of Tyre and Sidon.

And, behold, a woman of Canaan came out of the
same coasts, and cried unto him, saying, Have mercy
on me, O Lord, thou son of David; my daughter is
grievously vexed with a devil.

Matthew 15:21,22

This woman came to Jesus crying, "I have a devil-
possessed daughter, Jesus. Have mercy on me...Jesus, I
have a devil-possessed daughter. Have mercy on me. Jesus,
I have a devil-possessed daughter. Have mercy on me"

And I tell you, Jesus didn't honor that. He didn't accept
it initially, because the next verse says, **But he answered
her not a word** (Matthew 15:23a). He wouldn't even talk
to her, much less honor her faith. Then the Bible says...**his
disciples came and besought him, saying, Send her away;
for she crieth after us** (Matthew 15:23b).

But I also tell you that Jesus wasn't interested in sending
her away. He was interested in her believing that He was
God: **But He answered and said, I am not sent but unto the
lost sheep of the house of Israel** (Matthew 15:24).

Remember now, this woman had a devil-possessed daughter. **Then she came and WORSHIPPED him, saying, Lord help me** (Matthew 15:25).

The first approach didn't work because the Lord put her faith to a test. The Lord always puts your faith to a test. The Bible is a test. So she said, "Oh, well, Lord. I know you Jews call us Gentiles dogs. But it doesn't make any difference about that kind of stuff. That's just an old saying, you know. You're my Master, and I'm just telling you now, Jesus, the way it is. You're my Master, and I'm telling You that I've come to worship You, Jesus. And it doesn't make any difference what You say to me, I am bowing down before the One, the true and living God. You are the Master of my life, and I'm just going to worship You, Jesus, that's the way it is!" (Matthew 15:25,26, author's paraphrase).

Now, Jesus is standing there watching her. A few minutes ago, He wouldn't even talk to her. Now, are you ready for this? After standing there watching all this, Jesus answered and said unto her, "Because you believe I am God to the point that you will worship Me," **O woman, great is thy faith...**(Matthew 15:28a).

GREAT FAITH
• • •

Jesus said this woman's kind of faith is not just faith. He called it great faith. Jesus said, **O woman, great is thy faith: be it unto thee even as thou wilt** (Matthew 15:28). Her devil-possessed daughter was made whole from that very hour (Matthew 15:28b, author's paraphrase). And the daughter wasn't even present. Glory to God!

People ask me all the time, "Can you make devils leave someone at a distance?"

Are you kidding? The devil-possessed daughter was over in another village, but because the woman bowed down before God, and worshipped Him, and didn't take "no" for an answer, just worshipped God — Jesus said, "Your faith pleases Me." Then all of a sudden, His power shot over into another village, into the room where the devil-possessed daughter was, and drove all the devils out of her. Why? Because the mother bowed down before God and worshipped Him. Can you imagine how that mother felt when she went back home and her daughter who had been demon-possessed, sat up and said, "Hello, Mother, I love you...?"

So you say you have a need and say, "Brother Norvel; how do I get God to help me?"

Well, then, get this:

> But thou, when thou prayest, enter into thy closet, and when thou hast shut thy door, pray to thy Father which is in secret; and thy Father which seeth in secret shall reward thee openly.
>
> **Matthew 6:6**

Several years ago, the Lord said to me, "Son, tell My children to believe that I am God, and invite them to come to Me and worship." Then He gave me this Scripture, **He that cometh to God must believe that He is...** (Hebrews 11:6). If they'll believe that I am God — that is first, and then worship Me, because I am God — then, what I see My children do in secret, just alone in their secret place worshipping Me because they love Me as their personal God — I will reward them openly."

But now listen real close: If you're going to try to use God as a stepping-stone to get something from Him, you can forget it. God told me to tell you to spend time on your knees worshipping Him first before you ever ask anything. Just like the woman with the demon-possessed daughter, worship God, and He will honor your faith. Glory to God!

I Want A Camel!
• • •

If you are ever going to know how to please the Lord, you will need to know that the flesh, my brother, that body of yours, will drag you up and down every alley in town. Even after you get saved, you will never get in the will of God until you tell it "NOOOOO!" You will live out there, somewhere in God's permissive will, the rest of your life. And you will never know the divine will of Almighty God.

MORE POWER
• • •

After I gave my life completely to the Lord Jesus, I finally came in contact with the Full Gospel Businessmen, glory to God. And they started telling me about an experience I could have with God that would give me more power called the Baptism in the Holy Ghost with the gift of speaking in other tongues. I had already been serving God for some time in the ministry of helps and thought I had given Him my life completely. So the first time I heard about it, I thought, *Well, okay God, I give all of my life to You now,* and I thought that was it.

But the devil immediately said, "Tongues aren't real, that group is crazy, it's a cult. Why don't you leave and go back to your own kind?" I thought about it a while, and stayed.

So I kept on fooling around, and attending these businessmen's meetings. And I want to tell you, if you keep fooling around the Holy Ghost and His people, you will get so hungry for this experience that you will be willing to do whatever God asks. And I got it, glory to Jesus. Because I was amazed watching these businessmen praying for the sick and casting out demons. And I was amazed that people could be set free just by speaking Jesus' name, saying, "GO!"

But before I could receive God's supernatural power, the Lord had to deal with me in my spirit. *I'm either God or I'm not God*, He told me. *You either believe what I say or you don't. If you believe that I mean what I say, why don't you act like it?*

Then the Holy Spirit began to unfold the Scriptures that got me hungry. And after a while, I was so hungry for this experience that I began to beg Jesus to baptize me in the Holy Ghost. Day after day, I just kept on begging, but nothing happened.

BODY RULING, PLEASING FAITH
• • •

Well, this was before I quit smoking, and one day the Holy Spirit said, "I want you to stop smoking!"

So I said, "What's smoking got to do with it? I've been smoking for twenty years."

But Jesus said, "You want Me to baptize you in the Holy Spirit, so I want you to stop smoking."

So I said, "Oh, I didn't know it was that important to You, Lord. But if You want me to quit smoking, I'll take these Camels and I'll just lay them down." So, I just took the Camels out of my pocket and laid them down, and said, "Okay, I quit."

Well, glory to God, about three or four hours went by and my jaws began to ache. Then very nice and quietly my body said, *I want a Camel.*

You see, your body wants exactly what it's been used to. Eat three chocolate bars a day for a month, then try on the thirty-first day to stop, and see what your body does. About three o'clock in the afternoon your body will say, "I want a Hershey bar!" I'm not kidding. This goes on in the flesh of everybody who is addicted to anything.

I knew a young woman who was addicted to Coca Cola. She drank twenty-five cokes a day. That was in the day when cokes were in little bitty bottles. She would drink twenty-five a day, and she became addicted. Her addiction was so bad that she decided to go to the doctor.

After hearing her story, the doctor told her she was addicted and was going to have stop drinking cokes before they killed her. "But I wouldn't dare advise you to stop drinking cokes tomorrow," he said. "To do so would cause your body to go into shock. So tomorrow, I want you to start reducing the number of cokes you drink a day. On the first day, drink twenty-four cokes. On the next day, I want you to drink twenty-three. And on the next day twenty-two, and on down until you are down to one coke a day." Then he finally told her, "It will take you twenty-five days to get free of your addiction."

YOUR BODY WANTS WHAT IT WANTS
WHEN IT WANTS IT
• • •

Can you believe that? This woman's addiction was cokes and my addiction was cigarettes. And after I decided to quit smoking "cold turkey," my body wanted a cigarette. But I told it "No you don't. You can't have a cigarette because I've quit smoking." Still, my body said, *I want one anyway.*

It makes no difference what the addiction, your body wants what it wants, when it wants it.

Another eight hours went by, and my body rose up again — not quietly, but with a loud voice and said, *I want a Camel!* So I said again, "No! You can't have one." But my body was aching all over. I wanted a cigarette so bad I could hardly stand it. When I went downtown I would meet people on the street who were smoking, and you know how you pass them, and it blows in your face. So I would turn around and want to follow them. People who have never smoked, or who have never been an alcoholic or on dope, would never understand this.

Then finally one day, I just said, "No, body." But about the second day after that, I was fit to be tied. I mean my body was pounding and shouting at me, *I WANT A CAMEL, I WANT A CAMEL! I WANT A CAMEL! ARE YOU CRAZY? WHAT DO YOU MEAN FEEDING ME CAMEL CIGARETTES FOR TWENTY YEARS, THEN SUDDENLY CUTTING ME OFF? I WANT ONE. I WANT ONE. I WANT ONE!!!!*

I was a nervous wreck. I told my body, "*NOOOOOO,* you can't have a Camel!" Then just as plain, my body said, *THEN*

GIVE ME A CHESTERFIELD! "You've got to be kidding," I told it. You have to be desperate to want a Chesterfield.

It took a while, but my spirit won the battle over my flesh, and I am free from that filthy addiction. And I got baptized in the Holy Spirit. I couldn't do any of the things I do today without the Baptism of the Holy Spirit. The devil will tell you to go hide somewhere. And your body will fight you. But when you're not in control of your body, you will do all kinds of dumb things. So keep your spirit strong enough to tell your body what to do by reading the Bible, praying in tongues, and worshipping God every day.

Jesus may not tell you to quit smoking if you smoke before He baptizes you in the Holy Spirit. He may baptize you just to give you more power to quit smoking. But never let your spirit get so weak that your body orders you around. You can't afford it.

Servant Hearted Pleasing Faith
• • •

**James, a servant of God and of the Lord Jesus
Christ, to the twelve tribes which are scattered
abroad, greeting.**

**My brethren, count it all joy when ye fall into
divers temptations; Knowing this, that the trying
of your faith worketh patience.**

**But let patience have her perfect work that ye
may be perfect and entire, wanting nothing.**

James 1:1-4

Some time ago, I was in El Paso, Texas, holding a meeting, when God told me He wanted me to do something to
serve Him in a special way. I had been serving Him, I
thought, in the ministry for many years. So I asked, "God,
what do You mean, serve?" And as I waited before the
Lord, He said, "I want you to bring Rock Hudson your tape
series, *How To Live and Not Die.*

Rock Hudson was dying with AIDS in Los Angeles. So
this meant I would have to buy a plane ticket from El Paso
to Los Angeles. This was about five weeks before the
movie star died.

At that time, the only connection I had with Mr. Hudson
was Toni, one of his nurses. She was a beautiful black

Christian nurse who had appeared on the 700 Club. And she was one of Rock Hudson's nurses. So I got on a plane and went to Los Angeles.

I had been in touch with Toni about how God had been dealing with me to get these tapes to Rock Hudson and we agreed to meet. When we did, I found out Mr. Hudson didn't have a cassette recorder. So I bought him one, and Toni agreed to get the tape recorder and my tapes to him.

TONI
. . .

Toni would be the real servant in this situation. The next day she took my tapes and the tape recorder to work with her. She was on the night shift at that time. But when she brought them into Rock Hudson's room, he said, "I want to tell you something right now, Toni. I like you, that's the reason you're here. But I don't want anything to do with religion — nothing, understand? Nothing."

So Toni just agreed with him and left the recorder and my tape series, *How To Live and Not Die,* by his bed. When her shift was over, she took them home. Then when she would go back on duty, she would put them back beside his bed. Toni wouldn't say a word. She would simply walk in, and just put the tapes there every day.

Well, as you know, Mr. Hudson kept getting worse, and about two weeks before he died, Toni saw him looking at the tapes and the recorder. Then finally one day, he reached over, opened the case, and started listening to one of my tapes.

Later, Toni called me on the phone and said, "Norvel, he started listening to it, and I could tell he was real interested. After he had listened for a while, and he got to a certain point, I could tell it was time. So I just walked up to his bed and I said, 'Mr. Hudson, you know I'm a registered nurse, and I know about medical science. I know what can be done by medical science, and I know what can't. And Mr. Hudson, there is nothing medical science can do for you now. In fact, there is only one way that you could ever possibly be healed, only one way.'

"'What do you mean?' Mr. Hudson replied. 'The doctor says there's no way I can be healed.'

"'Well,' I said, 'there is one way, only one way.'

"'What's that?'

"Then God gave me just the right words to say, 'If God Almighty came down out of heaven, and touched you, you would be healed, that's the only hope for you ever to be healed.'

"'From what the doctors say, I guess you're right,' Mr. Hudson said. 'That's the only way I could ever be healed.'

"So I said, "Mr. Hudson, you know Jesus loves you, and He does great things for people that belong to Him.'

"'What do you mean?' Mr. Hudson asked.

"'I mean, He loves you,' I said, 'and He would like you to belong to Him. He wants you to come to heaven.'

"Finally he said, 'Well, Toni, I guess it's about time in my life that I started thinking about things like that.'

"'Yes sir, Mr. Hudson, it is that time. I would be glad to pray for you if you wanted me to. Would you let me pray for you?'

"'Well, uh...sure, if you want to.'

"Then I asked God to take away Mr. Hudson's physical pain, and led him in a sinner's prayer."

As Toni told me all of this, I stopped her, and said, "Now Toni, I can't share this testimony in public meetings unless I get it straight. Did you actually hear Rock Hudson ask Jesus to come into his heart?"

"Yes I did," she said. "He actually asked the Lord to come into his heart, and he received Him. And after he did, I saw a peace come upon him and he would smile and say, 'Well, I'm all right now...well, I'm all right now, I'm all right.'"

Elizabeth Taylor came to see Rock Hudson one day and Toni heard him tell her, "Liz, don't worry about me, I'm all right."

Toni told me how hard it was for all of Rock Hudson's friends to see him, a tall, handsome, talented man being eaten away by AIDS down to just a skeleton. But she also said when they would come the last two weeks of his life that he would reach out to them just like he did to Elizabeth Taylor. "I'm all right now," he told them. "Don't worry, I'm all right. I've made my peace...."

About two or three weeks after Rock Hudson died, an international magazine wrote an article about him that said, "Rock Hudson said in the last week of his life, 'Don't worry about me, I've made my peace with God.'"

Now this happened because a bold nurse named Toni, who had a servant's spirit, delivered my tape series, *How To Live and Not Die*, to Rock Hudson when he was dying with AIDS. She put it on the table beside him, every day.

Then she had enough godly wisdom to know when it was time to lead him in the sinner's prayer.

GOD IS PLEASED WHEN YOU BECOME HIS SERVANT
• • •

James, a servant of God and of the Lord Jesus Christ, to the twelve tribes which are scattered abroad, greeting.

James 1:1

When you become a servant of God, like Toni, you obey Him. It doesn't make any difference what it costs me, that's beside the point. When the Holy Spirit speaks to my spirit for any service, I want to obey Him. So should you.

IF YOU WANT TO PLEASE THE LORD, BE AVAILABLE
• • •

Be available to obey the Lord. I tell Him daily that I am available to go anywhere in the world to pray for one sick person. Or to cast the devil out of one person if He wants me to. All God has to do, is just tell me who and where they are, and what He wants me to do.

The day before Rock Hudson died, Pat and Shirley Boone called me out of my convention in Gatlinburg, Tennessee, to tell me Rock Hudson wanted to see me.

So I said, "Okay. All right. I'll be out there in about two days, are you kidding?" But the devil killed him the next day, just sitting there. He wasn't even supposed to die. He was supposed to live two or three more weeks. They said he got up, they put his clothes on him, he walked over to his chair, and he sat down. Then, all of a sudden, he just died.

The devil beat me to Rock Hudson before I could teach him on physical healing. But because of Toni's servant heart, he didn't get his eternal soul! Glory to God forever!

I have found from experience that if you show God you will help Him spread the Gospel, He will bless you so much you can't stand it. He will bless you with joy, and He will bless you with peace. He will give you boldness. And, you won't have nervous faith, glory to God. You will find that when you freely give your life to become a servant of God, a lot of those crazy things that have kept your faith from working will begin to drop off of you. And God will have another trusted servant to minister in this world.

Let God Walk in Your Shoes
• • •

**This people draweth nigh unto me with their
mouth, and honoureth me with their lips; but their
heart is far from me.**

Matthew 15:8

There are all kind of worlds, and I believe if you don't
like the world you live in, you can change it. You choose to
walk in one of the two worlds I talked about in chapter 1.
You can walk in the world of faith, or the world of reason.
The kind of world you live in depends on the strength of
your faith. If you are goofed up and in the world of reason,
the condition that put you there makes no difference, none
at all. Because God's mighty power in your life can change
the condition. You can walk in faith, but you have to choose.

Now I want to teach something out of the Gospel of
Matthew that will help you choose your world. You may
not like it, but it's in the Bible, glory to God. You know,
sometimes, if Bible lessons and sermons don't make you
mad, you don't get any help. God didn't call your pastor to
leave you in the condition he found you in. God called your
pastor to shake your brain every Sunday morning so you
can think straight, and start thinking in a heavenly way.

Heaven is a place of victory and God wants you to walk in victory. He wants you to enjoy a touch of heaven now.

Here it is; here is the verse that will help you choose your world: Jesus said, **This people draweth nigh unto me with their mouth, and honoureth me with their lips; but their heart is far from me** (Matthew 15:8).

What does that mean? It means your heart may belong to Jesus, but your life can belong to you if you won't lay it down for Him. It means you can choose to walk your own way, in your own shoes, go to church on Sundays, and live your own life. Or you can choose to walk with Jesus, in His shoes, and let Him be the Lord of your life.

FLOATING, JUST FLOATING ALONG CHURCHES
• • •

Many churches in America are full of people who in their heart basically belong to the Lord. They love the Lord to a degree, and they want to go to heaven because they don't want to go to hell. They believe that Jesus is the Son of God, and that God is real. And they believe in the virgin birth and the death and resurrection of Jesus. But they also believe their life belongs to them. They do what they want to, when they want to. And it doesn't make any difference to them what anybody thinks.

Most Christians have never won one soul to the Lord in their entire life. They have never brought a sinner to church. They don't pray for the sick. They don't help people when they're sick. And they don't help people when they're hungry. They just kind of float along. They find a church that can feed them, and just stay there all their life. Because God is merciful, He may give them a room in somebody's mansion in heaven. But when they die, they're going to be judged by the works they did while living in this body.

Why?

Because that's when we will all find out if we have been sold out to God, my brother.

YOUR BODY IS NUTS!
• • •

Now let me tell you something again about your body. Your body is only a house that your spirit lives in. And you can get your spirit in pretty good shape with God. You can read the Bible, and pray, and get close to God. But you have to put up with your body. And your body is nuts — it's totally crazy!

Your body doesn't ever want to pray. And it never wants to put on Jesus' shoes to go to the grocery store to buy groceries to feed the poor. In fact, your body doesn't want to do anything that it doesn't have to do. Are you kidding? The only reason your body even goes to work is because you have to live. If you would let your body have its way, it would just lay around all day, watch TV, and eat hot fudge sundaes.

Every time my body sees a coconut pie, it wants three pieces. But my spirit says, "You crazy thing, you don't get three pieces, what's wrong with you? Are you crazy? You'd get so big you couldn't get through the door." So I make a deal with my body and tell it, "I'll make a deal with you body. If you'll be real nice, I'll give you one big piece." But most of the time, my body wins.

SMOKE BREAK SUNDAY
. . .

If you want to know the truth about it, I never even thought it was wrong to smoke when I was growing up. In chapter 7 I told you the end of the matter. But I was brought up in a traditional denomination, and the men of that church smoked like a furnace. In fact, I think they invented it. When you're raised in Tennessee and North Carolina like I was, no one gives a second thought about smoking, because that's where they raise tobacco. Many families make their living raising tobacco as a money crop. You can make big money raising tobacco.

My daddy smoked, and my uncles smoked. All the men smoked. So we gave a smoke break in church. Every Sunday morning, Sunday school turned out at five minutes till eleven and the men would leave the church building real quick like to go out into the church yard. Then the moment they stepped out, they would light 'em up.

The Bible says you produce after your own kind. If you smoke, don't you know your little boys are going to want to smoke? They will think it's all right, because you do it. But if you don't smoke, they probably won't. So, I didn't think it was wrong. I saw my daddy and my uncles, and all the men of the church smoke, and I smoked for about twenty years. But when I really came to know the Lord, all that changed.

PLEASING FAITH
. . .

When the Lord called me to start living in His world of pleasing faith, I was an executive making around

$5,000.00 a week in my business. One night I came out of an executive meeting, and got in my Cadillac and started home. After driving about 175 miles through Ohio, I lived in Indianapolis, I don't know why, but I started to say a little prayer. And when I did, the Spirit of God came into me, and His Presence filled my car.

The Holy Spirit broke me open inside, and the Lord melted me for an hour-and-a-half as I drove down the highway. That was the night I gave my life to the Lord. He said, "I want to set you on a high hill. I'm going to set you on a high hill and the light of God will shine down from you to many men on earth. Come, follow Me."

I said, "Really, me? I'm a businessman. I thought You called preachers." So I gave my life to Him and worked in the ministry of helps for about seven years.

I didn't know God had a teaching ministry for me. I just worked in the ministry feeding the poor, helping little poor kids and trying to keep the high school kids off dope by putting on high school assemblies. I also helped build a little church over by the city dump for little kids that didn't have any money.

Then one day the Lord said, "I want you to teach for Me."

I said, "Are You kidding?"

He said, "No. I want you to start studying the Bible, son, on the subject of faith."

I had been teaching supervisors how to teach sales-men how to sell, but I didn't know God was ever going to call me to teach the Bible. If you want to know the truth about the matter, I didn't care about any of it. I didn't care anything about the kind of public ministry God has me in today. I was satisfied working with my own money helping little poor kids and poor families and high school kids in the ministry of helps.

Once I began to teach, I didn't even take an offering for seven years. What did I need an offering for? I had a business of my own. I wanted to give money to God — not take it from Him. But I found out that if you start working in the ministry of helps, if you start walking in Jesus' shoes, God will bless you so much you won't be able to stand it.

LET GOD WALK IN YOUR SHOES
• • •

God doesn't bless stingy or lazy people! If you're going to be one of those kind of human beings, you're on your own. You will never please the Lord. And you will never receive His blessing. So just get ambitious and start working for God. Tell your body to "shut up!" and start worshipping God every day. Tell your body that you're going to walk in Jesus' shoes and start bringing sinners to church.

"Wha — what? You mean God in *my* shoes?"

Oh, yeah! God, loves to walk in them. He loves to be in your shoes. And you will begin to understand that God loves busy people. Just get busy for God. Don't be one of those lazy Christians who draw near to God with their words, but their hearts are far from Him. Get busy with God.

Cancer Healing Pleasing Faith
· · ·

If any of you lack wisdom, let him ask of God, that giveth to all men liberally, and upbraideth not; and it shall be given him.

But let him ask in faith, nothing wavering. For he that wavereth is like a wave of the sea driven with the wind and tossed.

For let not that man think that he shall receive any thing of the Lord. A double minded man is unstable in all his ways.

James 1:5-8

Many times people say, "Brother Norvel, can you tell me why I can't..." but before they can finish, I say, "Oh yeah, I can tell you why. You're letting your faith waver, and when you allow that to happen, you won't receive anything from God. Are you kidding? I can't afford to let you *even think* you're going to receive from God if you let your faith waver." So I want to talk to you in this chapter about some of the things that can cause your faith to waver. But most importantly, I want to teach you how to received God's healing from cancer and how you can teach others to be healed.

That's right, I said cancer. Only Jesus can heal cancer. I am going to show you how God healed Hulda's cancer so He can heal cancer if you've got it. Or somebody else if they've got it. Because Jesus is the healer of cancer! Glory to God! It is His will to heal cancer!

HOW TO LIVE AND NOT DIE
. . .

There's nothing that can make a person's faith waver like cancer. Oh yeah. It will make you waver if you let it. So in God's world of faith, you have to know how to do things. This means you need His wisdom. And you need to ask for wisdom because the Bible says:

> **If any of you lack wisdom, let him ask of God that giveth to all men liberally, and upbraideth not; it shall be given him.**
>
> **But let him ask in faith, *nothing wavering*. For he that wavereth is like a wave of the sea driven with the wind and tossed. For let not that man think that he shall receive any thing of God of the Lord.**
>
> **James 1:5-7**

So what does that mean? It means to *ask* with *patience*. It's so pitiful when I walk in sometimes and see a person wasting away with cancer because he doesn't know how to minister the spiritual laws of the Bible. It has been only a few years since God gave me the ministry to teach people *How To Live and Not Die*. When He called me to do it, He said, "Son, walk into that cancer patient's room with your spirit full of patience and faith, and tell them just like it is." So that's what I began to do. That's what I did with Hulda.

HULDA
. . .

A millionaire friend of mine who lives in California called me one day and said, "Norvel, I have a secretary. You know, the black-haired Italian girl, Hulda. She's only in her thirties, has a child thirteen years old, and she's getting eaten up by cancer. They've operated on her twice. All of her hair's fallen out and they've sent her home to die. But after hearing you teach, I've been wondering, does she have to die with cancer?"

"You're wondering right," I told him. "She doesn't have to die."

So he invited Hulda over with her thirteen year old son, and the three of us had dinner together that night. After dinner, we went into the living room, and I learned Hulda had been told that she didn't have one chance in ten million to live. They said she had cancer from the top of her head to the bottom of her feet. She had cancer of the liver, cancer of the breast, and cancer of the kidneys. Cancer was eating her up.

I told Hulda right away that she didn't have to die, and that cancer was a lie from the devil.

Then I told her, "You don't have to die, Hulda, Jesus wants you to live. And I'm going to start teaching you right now how to live and not die. Is that all right?"

"Yes, oh yes," Hulda told me.

I told Hulda the teaching would take a while, and that I would take her through my six-tape series on, *How To Live and Not Die*. Then I shared with Hulda how the Lord showed me several years ago how people miss His blessing for not confessing His Word.

"Most of My children believe the Bible to a degree, and they love Me," the Lord told me. "But they miss Me and miss My victory because they don't speak My Word out loud."

I asked the Lord what He meant about the speaking part and He gave me an example.

"Have you ever heard a human being talking to the flu, holding a conversation with the flu?" the Lord asked me.

"No, Lord," I said, "I've never heard anybody holding a conversation with the flu."

Then He said, "Well, neither has any of the rest of My children. Many of them know nothing about it at all. But I plainly tell them in My Word exactly what to do. Every church has a Bible, and they read it. But only a few of them ever obey it, they just read it. They read it because it's a nice book."

I said, "What do You mean by that?" And He showed me a Scripture, and said, "I have already told My people what to do. I have said to them, whosoever shall say unto this mountain...'be thou removed....' But they don't talk to mountains, they talk to Me about their mountains, and that is unscriptural."

> For verily I say unto you, That whosoever shall say unto this mountain, Be thou removed, and be thou cast into the sea; and shall not doubt in his heart, but shall believe that those things which he saith shall come to pass; he shall have whatsoever he saith.
>
> Therefore I say unto you, What things soever ye desire, when ye pray, believe that ye receive them, and ye shall have them.
>
> **Mark 11:23,24**

When Jesus told me this, I said, "Lord, what do You mean by mountains?" And He said, "Son, anything that's bothering you at any specific time, that is your mountain."

Then I told Hulda the cancer that was eating her up — was her mountain.

"We're not praying for good blood, or good lungs, or whatever. We're dealing here with a cancer that is eating away at your whole body," I told her.

"Now pay attention closely, Hulda, because I want you to get this message so you will know how to talk to that cancer."

I told her I would pray first, and that she would pray later. Then I reached my hand toward her and said, "Now, *cancer,* I come against you in Jesus' name, and I curse your very roots. I curse your roots, *cancer,* and I command you to *die!* I command every root of this cancer in Hulda's body to *die!* Stop and wither away *cancer,* you disappear. I command it in Jesus' name!"

Then I told Hulda that it was her turn to pray.

"Now then, Hulda, that's my part. But now, I'm going to teach you how to talk to your mountain. I'm going to pretend that I'm you, and I'm going to walk the floor and say, 'Heavenly Father, I come to You in Jesus' name, and Your Word says that I have a right to talk to mountains. Jesus, You said in Mark 11:23 and in Matthew 21:21, **Whosoever shall say to this mountain, Be thou removed, and be thou cast into the sea,** You said that mountain would be removed. So Lord, the doctors tell me that I have cancer, and that I'm going to die with cancer. But I'm not going to receive that because I'm going to talk to it. So in the name of the Lord Jesus Christ, *cancer,* I'm talking to you right now, and I am telling you, *cancer*, I want you to listen to me, *cancer*. You understand, *cancer*, I'm talking to you. *Cancer*, I'm talking to you, not somebody else. I'm talking to you, cancer, and I'm telling you in Jesus' name, you aren't going to kill me. I'm telling you, cancer, in Jesus' name, you remove yourself from my body, and you be cast into the depths of the sea!"

Then I demonstrated cancer healing prayer again:

"*Cancer*, you go from me in Jesus' name. I don't want you, *cancer*. I resist you, *cancer*, and I am telling you, *go from me in Jesus' name!* I don't want you, and I'm talking to you. I'm not asking you anything. I'm telling you. Go from my body in the name of the Lord Jesus Christ. I'm not going to give you any choice. You don't have any choice. Jesus said in the Bible that whosoever shall say unto this mountain, **Be thou removed, and be thou cast into the sea, it shall be done for him** (Mark 11:23, paraphrase).

"So I say with my mouth, *cancer*, you remove yourself from me, and be cast into the sea. In Jesus' name, I don't want you. Remove yourself *from* me! Remove yourself from *me!* Remove yourself from *me!*"

I asked Hulda if she was getting it so far. And she said she was. So I told her getting it wasn't good enough because you can't heal yourself.

"The Holy Spirit Who lives inside of you is here on the earth to perform what the Bible says He will, Hulda. And we're going to put the Holy Spirit to work to start healing you today."

Then I prayed, showing her how again, "Now I'm going to walk the floor and say, 'Thank You, Lord, thank

You, Lord. I resist cancer and I command it to be removed from me. I'm talking to you, cancer. Remove yourself *from me!* Thank You, Lord, for doing it. Now, heavenly Father, in the name of the Lord Jesus Christ, I am Your child and the Holy Spirit lives in me, and the Holy Spirit does the work of God on the earth. Not somebody else — the Holy Spirit, and He lives in me.

'The Bible says that the Holy Spirit Who lives in me performs what He hears. And Holy Spirit, You hear me say right now that Jesus is my Healer, and the Lord Jesus Christ is healing me now. You hear me say that I believe in the healing power of the Lord Jesus Christ. You hear me say that the healing power of God is in my body now. The healing power of the Lord Jesus Christ is driving out all symptoms of cancer in my body.

'And Holy Spirit of God, You are healing me completely and making me whole and making me well, and making me free from all disease. You are healing me now. And I thank You, Lord, for healing me. I thank You, Lord, for healing me. I thank You, Lord, for healing me!'"

Hulda nodded her head when I asked if she got it again, so I said, all right, show me you have it.

Then I sat down, and she got up. I told her to start walking the floor just like I did, and speak to the mountain of cancer. So she started, "Oh. Oh, heavenly Father, in Jesus' name, ah, ah, I come to you, and I confess that You said that whosoever shall say to this mountain, be thou removed and be thou cast into the sea...."

I stopped her right there and said, "Wait a minute, wait a minute, Hulda, Hulda. You'll die if you do it like that. Hulda, you're saying about the same words that I said, but your words have no meaning, they have no power. God doesn't confirm and work with nonchalant faith. He doesn't work with nonchalant words. You can't say the words of the Bible any way you want to. You have to say them with power and enthusiasm. You have to say them like you mean it. Now, let's try it again."

"Okay..., Jesus, You said — You said whosoever shall say unto this mountain be thou removed and be thou...."

"No, no, Hulda, that won't work — here, give me your hand, and follow me. Do you understand what I mean when I say get up on the inside of you? Get up!"

Bless her heart, she was so weak, but she nodded, and I took her by the hand, and we started walking the floor together. I said again, "Jesus, You said whosoever shall say unto this mountain, be thou removed, be thou cast into the sea, go from me, it shall be done for him. Whosoever shall say to this mountain..., and I say, *cancer,* you depart yourself from me. You go from me because the roots of you have been cursed in Jesus' name, and you can't live in me. I'm talking to you, and I'm telling you, be removed from me, in Jesus' name!"

If you have a disease like cancer, it's so important when you come to the truth of confessing Jesus as Healer, that you do it for at least ten or fifteen minutes. Say nothing but, "Jesus, You are my Healer. Jesus, You are my Healer. Jesus, You are my Healer..." over and over and over and over. It will save your life! Not only will Jesus get the message that you believe it, but pretty soon, your inner man will get the message. And then the devil will get the message that his cancer has no part or place in you.

HAVE FAITH IN GOD'S WORD
• • •

Whatever you call Jesus, He becomes that to you. Not whatever you think He is, but whatever you call Jesus with your mouth, in reverence from your spirit, He becomes that to you. So if you're dying of a disease, make sure that you stick to that for ten or fifteen minutes two or three times a day, saying, "Jesus, You are my Healer. Jesus, You are my personal Healer. Jesus, I love You, and You are my personal Healer. My faith, Jesus, is in You. My faith is not in something else, it's in You, Jesus. You are my personal Healer. Jesus, You are healing me now. Your healing power is flowing through me. Jesus, it is — because it's free. It's free for Your church. It's a gift to Your church. It's a free gift that's already been paid for, and I receive your free gift."

"But now Brother Norvel," you may ask, "if I do that, do you really believe Jesus will hear me?"

Not only will He hear you, my brother, but if you will do it every day, He will come to your house and heal you. Jesus didn't talk just to hear His brain rattle and to hear His tongue flap. When He says something, He means it.

I'm telling you, if you're born again by the Spirit of God, and you're washed clean and white as snow, anything that Jesus says to you, you have a right to it. Have faith in God's Word. Blessed be the name of the Lord!

TELL THE DEVIL WHERE TO GO
• • •

Hulda isn't the only case I've worked with. I take cases all the time, where there's no hope. They are dying with cancer, and nearly all their flesh is gone, just skin wrapped around a body. And I work with them like I did with Hulda. The devil knows God uses me this way to get them healed. I get hold of impossible cases, but I'm telling you that the Lord God heals them when we tell the devil where to go.

Hulda, was dying with cancer, without hope or hair. She was dying! But she spoke to that mountain of cancer, and bound the devil every day, just as I taught her. I made her promise me to stay in there, every day! Every day! Every day!

Later, Hulda told me that she talked to that mountain of cancer for five months. She couldn't tell any difference at all in her condition until after two or three weeks. But at the end of the second week she knew she was getting better. And by the end of the second month she knew she was completely healed. Her hair began to grow out and she began putting on some weight, glory to God! Finally, in the fifth month, she knew she was completely healed.

Hulda was full of faith and would say to her mountain for about an hour or two in the morning, and sometimes an hour in the afternoon, "Jesus said, whosoever shall say to this mountain, be thou removed, so I say unto you, cancer, remove yourself from me, in Jesus' name. You've been cursed, and you can't live in me. You can't live in me. My body belongs to God. You can't live in me. What do you think you're doing, trying to take me over? You can't take anything over because you're dead, in Jesus' name. You've been cursed. And you can't live in me. You can't live in me. Jesus is my Healer. Jesus is my Healer. Jesus is my Healer. The Holy Spirit is healing me now. The Holy Spirit is healing me now!"

After eight months Hulda went back to the same hospital where she had been sent home to die. She dressed up real nice, her hair long and shinning black, walked into the offices where her doctors were, and said, "Hi."

Only one of the doctors recognized her. "You look like the Italian lady we operated on months ago," the doctor said. "But it can't be you, no way, you can't be Hulda."

Another doctor looked at her and said, "The Hulda we operated on has been dead for months."

Then another doctor asked Hulda her name. "My name is Hulda," she answered. "You doctors ought to know me like the back of your hand, you've cut me open twice."

"Oh, no. Nooooooo," they said. 'No. We've got the record over here. We all remember Hulda. We have the record over here. Our Hulda was totally eaten up with cancer. She's dead."

"What do you mean dead? I'm here. I'm alive!"

After a long, long, time, they said, "Hulda, you look like the specimen of health, but we won't believe it unless you let us open you up and see for ourselves."

Hulda thought they might become believers if they were convinced. So she said, "I took it twice before, and I can take one more time."

They scheduled surgery, and Hulda actually went back into the hospital so they could cut her open again. Oh, glory to God. And now listen to this — their medical records showed they couldn't find one trace of cancer anywhere! Glory to Jesus! They said, "What in this world happened to you? You're your normal size, your hair has grown out, and you look so beautiful. What happened?"

So Hulda told them about the minister from Tennessee who taught her to hook up with Jesus and cast her mountain of cancer into the sea. "He taught me how to talk," she told them.

"Is that right?" they asked her. "What do you mean *taught* you how to talk?"

"I'm telling you," Hulda said boldly, "the gentleman from Tennessee taught me how to talk. He spent over an hour and demonstrated how to walk across the floor, and speak to that cancer, and tell it to leave. I began to talk like he did, and the more I did what he taught me to do, the better I got, and finally that cancer left because I talked to it, in Jesus' name."

So the doctors finally said, "Well, whoever that man from Tennessee is, keep on doing what he said — because he's got the answer." Glory to God forever!

The only reason I have the answer is because God showed it to me in the Bible: **Whosoever shall say unto this mountain, Be thou removed, and be thou cast into the sea; and shall not doubt in his heart, but shall believe that those things which he saith shall come to pass; he shall have whatsoever he saith** (Mark 11:23).

Now some people come to me now and then and say, "Brother Norvel, I know a lot of people who talked to their mountains of sickness who didn't get healed." And I tell them, "I don't doubt that a bit." I know probably a thousand who didn't get healed, but they didn't do what Jesus said. They may have been talking, but they were doing their own thing. You can't be confessing God's healing Scriptures one minute, then flaking out the next by wavering in what the devil has convinced your reasoning to do. You can't do your own thing. You can't doubt. You have to believe and be patient when you act on your faith. All the time! Every day! Be patient! I'm telling you, if you're born again by the Spirit of God, and you're washed clean and white as snow, anything that Jesus' Word says to you, you have a right to it. Have faith in God's Word. Blessed be the name of the Lord!

You Start Talking to Your Mountain
* * *

So start talking to your mountain. If it's cancer, don't let that mountain take you over, you belong to God. It will take patience and perseverance, but you can have it. Put your hand on this book right now and pray this prayer:

Heavenly Father, give me patience in my spirit. O God, calm me down. Calm my mind down. Give me patience, in my mind, and in my spirit, that I would walk the floor every day, talking to my mountain in Jesus' name, telling it to be removed, and be cast into the sea.... Help me to act on my faith in God's Word knowing that it is Your Word, when I confess to my mountain, "Be thou removed, and be thou cast into the sea," it will go from me, disappearing from me, forever and I'll be free.

God, give me patience in my faith, that I will obey the Lord Jesus Christ, and I will walk the floor, and I will talk to my mountain, and I will claim Jesus as my Healer, and I will praise Him, and I will thank Him out loud, for healing me. I will do it every day. Thank You, Jesus, for setting me free, from all diseases! Thank You for giving my spirit, and my mind patience that I can believe God according to Thy Word! Amen.

Pleasing Faith Words Will Set You Free!
• • •

Probably the shortest sermon Jesus ever preached is in Matthew 15:10. It says, **And he called the multitude**, and the first thing He said was, **Hear and understand....** Then He said unto them, **Not that which goeth into the mouth defileth a man; but that which cometh out of the mouth, this defileth a man** (Matthew 15:10).What Jesus said was short, but powerful, glory to God. **What comes out of your mouth defiles you** (author's paraphrase, Matthew 15:11).

The only reason that you're sick today, my brother, is because the right words haven't been coming out of your mouth. Now listen real close! If you speak the right words, like Hulda dying from terminal cancer did, you, yourself, can get God to heal you. But, just like Hulda, you have to *learn* how to do it. Then after you learn how to do it, my brother, you will have to do it. And I mean do it diligently. You have to do it faithfully. You have to do it every day. Every day. Every day!

"But Norvel!" you say, "I don't have time to talk right words each day and get God's healing power out of the Book of St. Matthew, and St. Mark, Luke, and John. I need someone to pray!"

Is that right? Well then, let me say this again. God doesn't bless doubt and laziness! You may want to be healed, but until you understand this truth, you're not going to get it. There's no use in just wandering around and thinking, *Maybe, God in His goodness will help me someday.* "Someday" may be too late. God wants you to have faith in Him right *now!* Because *now* faith is the substance.

I don't mean you shouldn't ask for the prayers of others. God works through anointings and through the laying on of hands. But your pleasing faith words to God that speak out His healing power every day — diligently, every day! every day! can get God to heal you yourself.

Your eyes have to be set on Jesus like a flint of fire, and all the way to the end where you can't see anything but victory — only victory. No conditions, nothing but victory. And if you don't have that kind of faith, and that kind of determination, you won't get the victory.

If your legs are crooked and twisted, you have to look at your legs and say, "Legs, I command you to be straight and to be normal!" You have to repeat it, "Legs, I command you to be straight and be normal. I command you! I'm talking to you, legs. I command you to be strong and be normal! I command you!"

You do it. Not Brother Hayes, not your pastor, not Brother Hagin, not anybody else. Forget that. You have to do it for yourself.

There is no Scripture to cover the idea that others can get healing and all kinds of miracles for you. God works through the anointing and through laying on of hands. But after you get your healing through somebody else's praying, always remember this: If you don't pass God's test

of faith, and confession, and dedication, and worship —
you will lose your healing every time.

Why?

You can't keep your healing from God and remain
ignorant. God loves you, my brother, but He doesn't bless
ignorance. So if you want God to do anything for you, you
better get smart real quick.

There is nothing ignorant about God. You and me
pass that test pretty good, glory to God. But there is nothing ignorant about God. God doesn't deal in ignorance
with any human being. He deals only in the truth of His
Word. And the Holy Ghost who lives inside of you, is a
performer. Do you understand that? He's a performer, and
He will perform any verse of Scripture you will obey. So
don't pray about it to *see* if God wants you to have healing
or not. That's unscriptural.

"Well, Brother Norvel, I've been praying about it,
and...."

Don't Ever Agree With the Devil
. . .

No, I said, don't pray about it. That's unscriptural.
God doesn't answer prayers for people who have to pray
about the Bible. You can pray fourteen years if you want
to. The Bible is true before you ever pray, and it will be
true when you get through. And God will just be sitting
there, never changing, knowing nothing but victory.
Because faith has total victory, and God will give us
anything we want, according to His Word — that is, if we
ever get our mouths straightened out.

The things that come out of your mouth can defile you. They can rob and steal your health, your money, and everything you have. They can make you suffer, or they can bless you. It all depends on what you've been doing.

I can look at most anyone and tell you what they've been doing with their mouth. I can listen to them less than three minutes and they don't have to tell me what's wrong. I already know what's wrong with them. Their mouth doesn't speak the right kind of words. They confess to me all the things that are wrong with them. But my brother, the worst thing that you could ever do in your life is to confess what's *wrong* with you. When you do that, you agree with the devil. Don't ever agree with the devil. Don't do it.

GOD'S CONTRACT
. . .

Agree with God in faith and He will bless you, because it's like a contract from heaven to earth. Jesus said, **Have faith in God** (Mark 11:22). That means, have faith in His Word. God wrote the Bible and sent the Holy Spirit from heaven to earth to perform the Bible. Mark 11:23 says the Holy Spirit performs what He hears. But it all depends on what He hears from you. What He hears from you, He does for you. This is the reason a book like this is so important.

What are you confessing? You say, "Well, I'm confessing that we have a good church." Well, thank God for that.

Someone else says, "I'm confessing I have a good pastor, and that I love the Lord." Well, thank the Lord for that too. I'm glad you have a pastor, and I'm glad you love the Lord. That's the foundation of Christianity.

Then someone else says, "Well, I'm just confessing that the — that, you know, the Lord's will be done."

But now I say, "That's dangerous."

Let me explain. Now it's good to confess, where your daily life is concerned, the same prayer that Jesus prayed in the garden: "Not My will, but Thy will be done in My life."

But if you confess that kind of a prayer over every thing in life, the devil will sift you as wheat because you don't *know* God's will.

The Bible tells you God's will for your finances, healing, and miracles. It tells you what you can do about God's will through using Jesus' mighty name and through your faith confessions. And the Bible tells you that faith is not seen.

The Bible also plainly says you have a right to **call those things that be not as though they were** (Romans 4:16-21). And the Bible plainly tells you, through the Lord Jesus Christ Himself, that those things that come out of your mouth can defile, or destroy you: **Not that which goeth into the mouth defileth a man; but that which cometh out of the mouth, this defileth a man** (Matthew 15:10). Now listen — Jesus didn't say those things that go into your mouth could destroy you in this verse. He said it is those things that come out of your mouth that can defile you. They can destroy you. They can rob you from the blessing of God.

That broken, sick, beaten down, weak, confused kind of life that many of you may be in today, is totally opposite from the life that God's prepared for you. There's only one lifestyle, my sister, that God Himself has prepared for you through Christ Jesus — it's called the abundant life. Do you have abundance in your life today, my brother? If you don't, you're being robbed by the devil.

And the only reason you're being robbed by the devil is because you're ignorant of what God says. That's the truth. You might as well know it. The Lord said, **if you know the truth, the truth will make you free** (John 8:32, author's paraphrase). Jesus said the devil is here for three reasons: to kill, steal, and destroy. He wants to kill you, your relatives, all your friends, and all your children. The devil wants to steal everything the Holy Ghost has for the church, and he wants to steal it all away from you. He wants to steal the gifts of the Spirit from the church, (which he just about has). And He wants to rob you of everything that God has for you. Jesus said the devil is a thief and a liar. So you can't believe anything he says or does — nothing at all!

MOUNTAIN MOVING FAITH PLEASES GOD
· · ·

So, have you been talking to the flu? Have you been talking to your crooked legs? Jesus said, **Whosoever shall say unto this mountain, Be thou removed, and be thou cast into the sea...** (Mark 11:23). What is your mountain? Is it cancer like Hulda *had?* Is it your empty pocketbook? Your rent payment? Why don't you claim what is right-fully yours? Tell that filthy devil to take his hand off your money. Say, "You flake, let go of my money, in Jesus' name." Claim it for yourself. It doesn't matter whether you have cancer or a twisted leg, or a bad kidney. Start resisting that demon. In Jesus' name, say, "No you don't!

Not to me. No you don't! I resist you. I resist you. I resist you. I resist you!"

Do it. Resist the devil. Resist conditions in Jesus' name. Resist him with authority. And do it continually, until in Jesus' name, you break the devil's power over you.

Patient Pleasing Faith
• • •

The Book of James says, **The trying of your faith worketh patience** (James 1:3). So faith has patience all the time, because faith is always tried. You may not think that's good, but God does, because patience pleases the Lord.

Sometimes, the longer God waits to give you the manifestation of what you're praying for, the greater the benefit. As you wait on the Lord, you will see the greatest things in the world begin to happen. Especially if you don't allow your faith to waver. All the time you're waiting, you're practicing, and practicing, and you're thanking God, and praising God, and believing God. If you refuse to waver, I will guarantee you, the next time you come upon something you have to use your faith for, you won't be trying to find every evangelist in the country to pray for you. Because when you practice your faith for yourself, you build your faith muscles.

It's good to have people pray for you, but did you know that you can get God to do anything you want for yourself? Did you know that? Well, I'm telling you boldly that you can. God loves you, my brother, and He will do anything for you *personally.*

Several years ago I asked God this question about unanswered prayer: "What about these people who have memorized the whole Book of Hebrews, and they say they have great faith, but You don't answer their prayers?" I asked. "What's wrong, Jesus?"

Well, the Holy Spirit unfolded it to me. Sometimes the Holy Ghost will move upon me and unravel the Word of God right in front of my eyes. He does that for the office of the teacher, because He wants the teacher to teach His truth. And He did that when I asked this question.

The Lord told me, "Some of My children pray and ask Me for something, and want Me to give it to them yesterday. But I won't do that, because sometimes, they aren't ready for what they ask. So I want you to teach them this way — I want you to teach the people to worship Me. Then, I want them to become My servants. I want them to serve Me and obey Me. And then, I want them to have joy in their life all the time."

GOD DOESN'T ANSWER NERVOUS PRAYERS
. . .

Then the Holy Spirit taught me that God's servants must learn patience, because God doesn't answer nervous prayers. He told me the more we worship Him and the more we praise and thank Him for whatever we're asking Him for, the better we will be able to understand His timing.

You know in some cases, God has His timing. He really does. But you need to learn that about God and quit trying to make God do things now. You can't make God do anything. So start learning to believe God by faith, with patience, joy, and thanksgiving.

LET PATIENCE HAVE HER PERFECT WORK
• • •

People are always asking me, "Brother Norvel, could you tell me how I could get myself to the place that I won't be *wanting* everything? I'm always wanting this, and I'm always wanting that, and nothing seems to work."

Oh yeah! We've all been there. But I can tell you how to change that. If you will get your spirit, your own human spirit, and your own human mind, full to overflowing with patience, you can have anything you want — it's easy. You just need to learn what the Lord Jesus Christ said. He said, **...take my yoke upon you, and learn of me; you'll find my yoke is easy and my burden is light...** (Matthew 11:29, author's paraphrase).

So it's not hard for you to get something from God. But when you wrestle with God, and wrestle with this, and wrestle with that, you won't get patience — you will only get worn out. Instead, learn to wait before God. Find a promise in the Bible that you need, and claim what you want from Him. Then approach Him with **patience.** And thank Him with **patience.** And **wait** before God. And do it with **thanksgiving** and **patience.** If you will do it, this is what the Lord says, **patience has the perfect thing to perform in you** (James 1:4, author's paraphrase).

The Bible says to **...let patience have her perfect work, that ye may be perfect and entire, wanting nothing** (James 1:4). What do you mean wanting nothing? If you will let your spirit and your mind be possessed with patience for a few years, and make this be your way of life, you won't be wanting anything, because you will have everything.

"Is that right?"

That's right. I said you will have everything. And you will have to stop and wonder, *Is there anything that I want? I have so many things, God's blessed me with so many blessings, now let me think.* You will have to wrestle with your own mind and have to think for a long time to think of even one thing that you don't have. God will give you everything you want. He will totally saturate you with blessings, because God says:

> And all these blessings shall come on thee, and overtake thee, if thou shalt hearken unto the voice of the LORD thy God.
>
> Blessed shalt thou be in the city, and blessed shalt thou be in the field.
>
> Blessed shall be the fruit of thy body, and the fruit of thy ground, and the fruit of thy cattle, the increase of thy kine, and the flocks of thy sheep.
>
> Blessed shall be thy basket and thy store.
>
> Blessed shalt thou be when thou comest in, and blessed shalt thou be when thou goest out.
>
> Deuteronomy 28:2-6

IT ALL COMES THROUGH PRAISE AND PATIENCE
• • •

It all comes through praise and patience, my brother. And always remember this: Stop that nervous business, or the devil will try to keep your thinking flaky. Always praise Him and He will bring the patience you need in your own faith.

"Action" Pleasing Faith
• • •

> And, behold, a woman, which was dis-eased
> with an issue of blood twelve years, came behind
> him, and touched the hem of his garment:
> For she said within herself, If I may but touch
> his garment, I shall be whole.
>
> Matthew 9:20,21

If you have the voice of victory and the voice of faith, you will also have *action faith*, glory to God. Because faith without action is dead. And faith that reaches out and touches Jesus with the voice of victory is action faith.

Here, in the Book of Matthew is a woman who was dying from disease and had no hope. But she pushed her way through the crowd, saying, **If I may but touch his garment, I shall be whole** (Matthew 9:21). Glory to God, she walks into this crowd and says, "If I can touch His garment, I'll be made whole. If I can just touch His hem, I'll be whole."

This is called action faith, my brother. You have to have action, my sister, not just faith. Get that straight, because God will honor that kind of faith.

I don't care if you're dying with cancer. All you have to do is touch Jesus. When you press in to seek Jesus with an affliction, when you walk the floor in prayer, saying, "Jesus! Jesus! You are my Deliverer, Jesus! You are my Healer!" And tell the devil "NOOOO!!!" This is action faith that is pleasing to God.*

GOD'S VIRTUE FLOWS INTO THOSE WITH ACTION FAITH
. . .

When this woman reached out and touched the hem of Jesus' garment, virtue went through her and she knew she was healed, glory to God. And Jesus knew that virtue went out of Him. But now get this: When she touched Jesus, He turned around looking, and asked, "Who touched Me, who touched Me?"

So the disciples said, "You've got to be kidding, Jesus. There's hundreds of people around here — a lot of people touched You!"

But Jesus said, "No, no, no, no, no, no, no! Somebody touched Me with faith and action. Somebody touched Me with faith!"

Then this woman looked up at Jesus, trembling, knowing she was healed, and Jesus said, "Lady, your faith has healed you!" ...**Daughter, be of good comfort; thy faith hath made thee whole.** And the Bible says ...**the woman was made whole from that hour** (Matthew 9:22).

---

*You can read more about this woman's whole action faith miracle in my book, *Your Faith Can Heal You.*

ACTION FAITH HAS A VOICE OF VICTORY
. . .

> And Jesus stood still, and commanded him to be called. And they call the blind man, saying unto him, Be of good comfort, rise; he calleth thee.
>
> And he, casting away his garment, rose, and came to Jesus.
>
> And Jesus answered and said unto him, What wilt thou that I should do unto thee? The blind man said unto him, Lord, that I might receive my sight.
>
> And Jesus said unto him, Go thy way; thy faith hath made thee whole. And immediately he received his sight, and followed Jesus in the way.
>
> Mark 10:49-52

Blind Bartimaeus was sitting by a road when the Lord came by, and Bartimaeus began to reach out with his *voice,* saying, "Jesus, son of David, have mercy on me! Master, son of David, have mercy on me!" And he kept on and on and on and on and on. The disciples tried to get him to stop, but he said, *"NO!"* And he kept on and on, saying, "Son of David! Jesus, have mercy on me!" He kept on and on and on and on.

ACTION VICTORY FAITH KEEPS
ON AND ON AND ON AND ON
. . .

Even after the crowds **charged him that he should hold his peace** (v. 48), Bartimaeus wouldn't stop. Instead, he said, "He's the One I want to see! He's the One I'm crying after! He's the One I need! Jesus! Jesus! Have mercy on me! Jesus! Have mercy on me! Son of David! Have mercy on me!"

The Bible even says, **He cried the more a great deal, Thou son of David, have mercy on me** (v. 48). It says he cried out louder, and louder, and stronger, and stronger. "Jesus, have mercy on me. Jesus, have mercy on me. JESUS, HAVE MERCY ON ME!!"

Bartimaeus wouldn't listen to those who wanted him to "show some reverence, and hold his peace." And if you will stop listening to human beings and religious organizations, and turn your face toward heaven, calling out to Jesus with the voice of victory, you will see that God is pleased with that.

You don't have the time to sit around with people who say, "Let me explain to you about the sovereignty of God. And let me explain to you about some of these cases...you know, some of these cases, ah, you know, well, I mean we just can't understand everything. We just, you know, can't understand why these things happen...."

God's either God, or He's not. And there's no use of you trying to wrestle with Him in your own sick mind for a reason why God didn't heal some person you know. You've got to be kidding.

I wondered for a long time why my mother died of cancer at the age of thirty-seven. And eventually, God told me the truth about the matter. It took me three days to get Him to tell me, but He did. He said: "She went to the wrong church."

My mother was never taught what I'm teaching you here. People only believe what they've been taught. But if you stayed around me very long, you would believe it. Oh, yeah, you would. After a while, you would get to the point that you believed God would do anything for anybody.

Wondering in your own mind why God is making you wait so long isn't faith. And reasoning isn't faith. If you want to know the truth about it, that will just keep God from paying any attention to you at all.

This woman and blind Bartimaeus refused to take anything except victory for an answer. Their message to you is: The God kind of faith keeps on with the voice of victory and keeps on with action until the manifestation comes. It keeps on with your voice of victory in the Lord Jesus Christ. Not someone else's, not your pastor's, not your friend's. No, *your* voice of faith keeps on with the voice of victory in the Lord Jesus Christ. And when you have that kind of faith, action voice of victory faith that believes God will do what He says, God will honor your faith.

CHAPTER 14

Demon Casting Pleasing Faith
• • •

One night the Holy Ghost came upon me in a shopping center and said, "Norvel, go to a certain city at a certain address." So, I got in my car and I drove there. When I arrived, I saw a demon-possessed college boy. He had lost his mind and didn't even know his own name.

So I asked the person in charge to lock me up in a room with him. They were only too glad to oblige. Locked up with the kid in that room, I prayed and bound the devil all night long. I said, "COME OUT OF HIM!" I command you to turn his mind loose! You're not going to keep this boy's mind! I've been sent here by God Almighty under direct orders from heaven, and I've come here to get this boy's mind back for him. You're not going to keep his mind. I'm not going to let you have him!"

I kept my action faith voice of victory working all night long.

"I know, Satan," I commanded, "that you want his mind, but you can't have him! I'm telling you, you can't. In Jesus' name, I'm telling you what you can't do, and you can't have him! I've come to get his mind back for him. The God I know is a miracle-working God, and God has sent me here under direct orders to pray for this boy in Jesus' name. OBEY ME! COME OUT OF HIM!"

About daylight the next morning, I broke that thing, and white foam began to bubble up out of that young man's mouth onto the floor. Then all of a sudden, he sat up and made a crazy kind of noise, and in seconds he was normal. The Bible calls it, ...**Clothed, and in [your] right mind** (Mark 5:15). He was perfectly normal, glory to God!

If you think you are going to break demon power in an instant by just saying, "in Jesus' name," I have news for you. You have to stay there, my brother, with the voice of victory, and let the devil know who you are in Christ Jesus. You have to let him know the power that is in Jesus' name. You have to have action faith, "demon-loosing" faith in God, and faith in the name of the Lord Jesus Christ. You must say NO to the works of hell and *claim* the victory for the demon-possessed person, in Jesus' name. Glory to God! You need to do that, just like I do it.

ZONA
. . .

My daughter Zona married Bobby when they were only eighteen. God told me they shouldn't get married, but they did it anyway. And almost immediately after they did, Bobby was drafted into the Vietnam War.

Zona was a faithful young wife, and never missed a day writing to Bobby. But I will never forget the day Zona came running and screaming through the house — I didn't know what had happened, and I couldn't stop her. She just kept running and screaming. Then I picked up the letter she had thrown aside. It read:

Dear Zona:

I don't want you anymore. This letter is to set you free from our marriage...you can do anything you want to do. I will never see you again....

I learned later that Zona read only the first part, and thought it was a "Dear John" letter. But I read further, and it said:

I'll never see you again...I'm going to die, I know I'm going to die. All of my buddies have been killed trying to crawl through these stinking swamps. At night we have to pick off these blood sucking leeches before we can get any sleep. But there's really no sleep...there's no way a human being can do this for very long. And I know of no way to get out of here....

From that very day, my daughter changed from a sweet, loving, Christian, to a demon possessed being. She started taking dope and running with a gang in our town, and the next three years of our lives would be a living hell.

After about a year of all this crazy stuff, Bobby came home. When he drove into the driveway, I met him, but all I wanted to do was get hold of him and thrash him. The love of God wouldn't let me do that, so instead, I said, "Bobby, I need to talk to you before you go in. You're not going to see the same girl that you left."

Then I asked him a question, "Bobby, why in the world did you write Zona that crazy, stupid letter?" He just stared at me in unbelief. So I said, "After she read the first paragraph, she threw your letter down and began running through the house screaming at the top of her voice. And at that moment, the devil came into her. She took off with a gang of dope addicts, and she's been with them ever since."

Bobby didn't say a word. So I continued, "I've had to put up with this since the day you wrote that stupid letter! I've been praying and binding up devils, and everything else. But you're not going to see the same girl that you saw before."

Finally, Bobby said, "Well, er I — I — uh, Mr. Hayes, I was on dope, and I thought I'd never see Zona again. And I didn't want to wreck her life. I mean, uh, I — I — I wanted her to be free, after I got killed, to marry somebody else if she wanted to, and to have a life.

"I — I — I never thought that I'd ever come back. Mr. Hayes, it's an awful thing to be with your best buddies one minute, crawling on your belly in the water, in the muck, and the snakes, and the leeches are up to your neck, and snipers are shooting, and you're trying to spot one, and shoot back. Then, all of a sudden, you don't hear anybody beside you, and you look over, and there is your best buddy laying over there with half his face gone.

"After I went through that for months and months of crawling in the swamps every day, and seeing so many of my buddies getting killed, I started taking drugs to try to have a sane mind. So, I just wrote Zona that letter."

"Well, I want you to know, Bobby," I said, "when you wrote that dumb, stupid letter, you wrecked Zona's life."

Then he said, "Mr. Hayes, I love Zona so much," could I please see her?"

I agreed, but told him, "You won't want to see what you will see, Bobby. You're not going to see the sweet, little Spirit-filled girl you left. You know, that's the way I raised her, and that's the way you married her. But that's not what you will see. Instead, you're going to see a demon-possessed creature from another world."

He looked at me with unbelief, and said, "Well, can I just see her?"

"Go on," I said, "she's back there in her room."

We went into Zona's bedroom, and she was sprawled on her bed. After staring for a few seconds, Bobby finally said, "Hi!"

But she looked up and told him, "You, you make me sick." When Bobby saw her condition, he knelt down by the bed in a position of prayer. And when he did, Zona just stepped over the top of him, walked out of the house, got in her car, and left. She didn't come back all night long.

I told Bobby this wasn't anything unusual. And that sometimes I wouldn't see her for two weeks. Sometimes I would see her on the street. Sometimes she would speak, and other times she wouldn't. Sometimes she would come home after being gone for two weeks and bring four or five girls with her, all of them on drugs.

Bobby looked at me in total despair, and I didn't see him again for a long time.

DO THE 'FUNKY' CHICKEN
• • •

I never will forget the day when five or six of Zona's friends came out. They were all in hot pants (very short skirts that were in style back then). I was out on the back porch, and one of Zona's friends came out and said, "Oh, Mr. Hayes, your daughter can really dance."

"Is that right?" I said.

"Oh, yeah," she went on, "we go to the Playmate Club all the time, you know, where they have the girls in the cages and the bands and everything. And every time they see Zona coming in, the band stops and they say, 'Here comes Zona,' then they start playing, and Zona begins to do the 'Funky Chicken.' Everybody at the Playmate Club likes to see Zona do the 'Funky chicken.'"

I said, "Funky Chicken, what's a Funky Chicken?"

"Well, that's the name of a dance, Mr. Hayes. All generations have certain types of dances," the girl went on. "You know, back in your day it was the Charleston."

"No, it wasn't the Charleston," I argued. "I wasn't a teenager back in the '20s. In my day it was the Jitterbug, not the Charleston. How old do you think I am?"

"Oh, well, I mean, you know," she said, "today it's 'Mashed Potatoes' and the 'Funky Chicken.'"

Finally I told her with a voice of victory, "Well, little darling, I've got news for you, and Zona, and everybody else who needs to know it. I have attacked my daughter's condition with my prayers of faith, and I'm not going to let my faith waver. My daughter is never going to go to hell. I'm claiming her soul, in Jesus' name. I'm putting my faith to work, and I'm not wavering. Do you understand me, little lady?"

She giggled a silly little giggle and said, "I guess so."

"And I'm telling you right now," I said while looking straight into her eyes, "My faith is going to work. And one of these days, Jesus is going to show up, and when He shows up, He's going to 'funky' my daughter's chicken!"

"Oh, really?" she answered.

"Really," I said.

Things got a little quieter after that. Then I said, "Do you remember the young man who owned the clothing store downtown, a real sharp young man?"

She nodded and said, "Yeah."

"Well, I used to go in his store and buy clothes from him," I went on. "He had a real exclusive men's store downtown. Had it all decorated and everything, but he started running with Zona and you all, and the other night he died of an overdose of drugs. And I'm telling you right now, my daughter is not going to die! The devil's not going to kill her! I'm claiming her in Jesus' name!"

Then this girl said in a shaken up low tone, "Oh," and left.

Well it wasn't very long until another one died. And then another, and another until five of them had overdosed on drugs. Five young people in one small town died, overdosing on drugs. They weren't gangsters. They were just on dope. Most of them were basically half-way decent kids. But they were just on dope, and it killed them.

ACTIVE FAITH KEEPS ON AND ON
• • •

My daughter wouldn't go to church, but I just kept on claiming her, and I kept putting my faith to work. Through it all I learned *again* that you have to put your faith to work if you want God to show up. It doesn't matter what it's for, you have to just keep active in putting your faith to work.

As I prayed and sought the Lord, I remembered how I stood in the gap for Zona when she was afflicted with horrible growths and boils. And how the Lord overshadowed and healed her — totally healed her! I remembered how new skin came upon her. And how the Lord removed every growth from her, just like that, as quick as you could bat your eye, and she was healed.

But now, years later, she was on drugs, and it seemed like I couldn't reach her. So I kept reminding her, "Zona, don't you remember how the Lord healed you and was so good to you to put new skin upon you and heal you? But now, you don't even go to church. You know you ought to serve Him the rest of your life. Not only did He heal you, Zona, He died on the cross to give you a new life, and bring you healing. You ought to serve God the rest of your life." Zona was not only on dope, she was also afflicted with a full-blown case of anorexia, and was taking up to ten boxes of laxatives a day.

NO MATTER WHAT YOU ARE FACING
GOD IS GOOD
. . .

But during this time, I continued faithful to God in my witness for Him, and I was on a television show telling how the Lord removed all those growths from Zona's body. Later, Pat Boone's wife, Shirley, called me and said, "We were sitting there watching you, and thank God, our daughter Cherie was watching too when you were on television, Norvel.

"Then when you told how the Lord came and removed all those knots and growths off of Zona's body, and put new skin upon her, our daughter was sitting there with anorexia, just like your daughter had. She was beginning to get growths on her body too. The devil was trying to kill her. And when you said, 'Stretch your hand out toward the television screen — I'm going to pray for you and I'm going to curse those growths in Jesus' name' — Cherie got up and walked over to the television set. Then she knelt down and put her hands on the television screen, and said, 'I agree with Brother Norvel in Jesus' name.'

"She had given her life to the Lord, Norvel," Shirley told me in thanksgiving to God. "But she still had anorexia. And when you cursed those things in Jesus' name, and commanded them to disappear, the growths disappeared off of Cherie's face."

Glory be to God forever. It pleases God to work miracles of healing right in the middle of the devil's mess. God was still showing Himself strong, and I just kept on praying and putting my faith to work.

Zona didn't want to have anything to do with Bobby whatsoever, and finally divorced him. But at night, I would walk the floor and make intercession, and worship God, and make intercession and pray, and confess in English, and say, "Satan, you'll never send my daughter to hell. In Jesus' name I say, you'll never send my daughter to hell! You're not going to drag my daughter to hell. I bind you in Jesus' name. I claim her soul for heaven in Jesus' name!"

And because I know it pleases God when His children speak to Him in tongues, I would pray in English, then in tongues.

CHAPTER 15

Never Changing Pleasing Faith
• • •

You may want to take a deep breath before I tell you how long I prayed for my sweet daughter Zona. How long you ask? Three years. And while I was praying that Zona and Bobby would get back together, they got a divorce. Zona would have nothing to do with Bobby. She got even wilder. I would try to get her to go to church, and she wouldn't go. For three years, I just kept on claiming and kept on claiming and kept on claiming with my voice of victory and action faith.

After about two-and-a-half years, the Lord told me one day while I was driving down the road, "The thing you want most of all is not going to happen until you change."

I said, "What do You mean, me change, Lord? Zona's the one who needs to change."

"No, You are not loving your daughter just like she is," He said. "So from now on I don't want you to keep lecturing her with your 'fatherly wisdom.' I only want you to tell her two things. Tell her 'I love you.' And tell her, 'Jesus loves you.' That's all you tell her. And then you be quiet."

So Zona would come in at two or three o'clock in the morning, and I would say, "Zona, I love you, honey, and Jesus loves you." Then I would make myself shut up.

After six months of this, the Lord said, "Do it all the time." So I would do it all the time, all the time, all the time! When she would come in late, I would just say, "Zona, I love you, Honey, and Jesus loves you. Zona, I love you little darlin', and Jesus loves you. Jesus loves you, little darlin'."

She would lay in her room, probably taking redbirds (a form of drugs) or smoking marijuana, and I would knock on her door and say, "Hey, Zona, I just want to tell you, Honey, that I love you; I love you, little darlin'."

FIRST SPARK
· · ·

I never will forget the day when I saw the first little spark of light, glory to God. About six months had gone by, and up to that time, Zona was hard as nails. I couldn't reach her. Forget that part. I just couldn't reach her.

Then late one Friday afternoon, Zona was sitting in the living room. She waiting on the gang to take her to the Playmate Club when she said, "Daddy, I know th...that you've taught me right, and I know the people I run with don't love me, they don't love anybody but themselves, that's all."

I just stood there, dumbfounded, and she went on, "And, Daddy, I'm getting to the place where I hate to go anywhere. I love this house, and when I'm here, I feel secure. There's no security in the world...my mind keeps wondering all the time. Most of the time I'm broke, and I don't have any money to buy dope and, and I try to do this and that, and nothing is working for me.... Daddy, I know I — I know that you love me."

I said, "Yep, you got that right, Honey, I do love you." I wanted to say so much more, but decided it was better to just listen.

"Daddy, I'm getting tired of my friends, they're all so phony."

"Well," I said, "I could have told you that. The devil's phony. Everything about the devil is phony. I could have told you that two-and-a-half — three years ago." I heard myself starting to "preach," so I just said, "Well, Zona, you don't have to go with them. You can make a decision now, you don't have to go with them. You know they're going to pull up in the driveway in a few minutes, but you don't have to go."

"But, they're looking for me, and I've already promised I'd go."

"Zona, don't go, Honey, don't go. You don't have to go — if you like this place and you feel secure here, you feel peace here, just stay right here."

"Well, yes, I know...."

About that time, the "devil" pulled up in the driveway, and she said, "Well, that's them, Daddy. I guess I'd better go."

The hardest thing I've ever done, was to stand there and let her go.

When she did, I just did the same thing I had been doing. Faith doesn't ever change! I began to walk the floor. And as I heard that hot rod with the gutted muffler go roaring out of hearing, I *continued* to walk the floor. And I said, "Satan, you devil, I bind you, Satan. I bind you, Satan, you can't have my daughter!"

And I kept on repeating my command to the devil to take his hands off Zona. When you keep on and on and on, and you don't waver, that is called faith.

And always remember, without faith, it's impossible to please God (Hebrews 11:6). That's another way God can approve your faith. You keep on and on and on and on and on, claiming what's in your spirit.

I kept praying and praying and praying that day. I walked across the living room floor, back and forth, to and fro, walking and praying and praying and walking, and telling the devil, "My daughter will never go to hell."

Well, walking the floor was nothing unusual for me, I had been doing it for three years. And when I saw a little spark of light that day in Zona, I was inspired to keep on. I mean I was binding the devil in Jesus' name. I Kept walking and praying and making intercession.

Then all of a sudden, the Word of the Lord come unto me saying, "You never have gone into her room, and put your hands on her bed, and prayed where she sleeps."

I said, "Oh!" That's right; I never have done that." So I ran into her room right quick, and I said, "I lay my hands on this bed in Jesus' name. Lord, I pray that You will shake her up; You will shake her up!"

Then I remembered when right before she left that day, that I asked her, "Zona, what would God have to do, Honey, to get you to follow Him again?"

She said, "I don't know, Daddy, shake me up, I guess."

So I said, "Well, God can shake you up, you know."

"Well, I guess He'd have to," she said.

Because I remembered what she said, the Holy Ghost started praying through me that way. I would bend over her bed and pray, "God, shake her up. I give my daughter to You, Jesus. When she lays in this bed tonight, shake her up, God, shake her up. Shake her bones, Lord, shake her up. I give her to You totally, Lord. Don't be nice to her. Shake her up. Shake her up."

I prayed loud and strong like that, glory to God forever. Then one night after I had prayed until 2 AM, Zona never came in, so I went on to bed.

Then, something woke me up in the middle of the night, and I heard a teeny, little voice. It sound like a mouse, or something. It went, "Eeeeeee, eeeeee, eeeeee," and it got a little louder, "EEEEE, EEEEEEEE!!"

"What's that?" I asked myself. "It sounds like a mouse, way off somewhere." Then I heard the same little voice, "Da — deeee, daaa-deeee."

"Daddy?" I said. "I only have one child, but that doesn't sound like Zona."

Everything in my room was just as quiet as it could be. I got up out of bed and opened my door, and Zona was standing there shivering, with that little squeaky voice coming out of her saying, "Daaaa-deeeee, daaaa-deeeee, daaaa-deeeee, daaaa-deeeee."

"Zona? What are you doing?" I asked her.

"Daaaa-deeeee, daaaa-deeeee, me, eeee, ma — man — a man, no, not a man, me, me, me, me, me, me, my room, my room, daddy, my room, daddy, man, man, me, me, not a man, me, me, meeeee."

111

She couldn't stop shaking. So I finally took her in my hands, and said, "Zona, Zona, stop it. Stop, Zona, talk to me. What are you trying to tell me? In Jesus' name, be calm."

Well, she kept shaking. I have never seen a human being that scared in my life. But I finally got her calmed down.

"Daddy, Daddy, Daddy, uh, uh, uh, there's a man in my room. There's a man in my room. I mean, he looked like a man. He was big, as two men, and taller than the ceiling He could have killed me. Daddy, he could have killed me, don't you understand that?"

Then, I remembered, she didn't know I had been praying in her room, so I told her, "Zona that wasn't a man in your room."

But she said, "Oh, Daddy, oh yeah. Yes, it was."

I said, "No, no it wasn't a man, that was your angel."

"Oh, no, no, Daddy, I don't want him here, he's too big; he scares me."

"I don't care if you want him or not, Honey, that's your angel; and he goes with you everywhere."

Then she screamed, "Daddy, don't say that! He scares me; don't say that!"

"Well, I am saying it. He's your angel, and he goes with you everywhere."

Now, I know I'm talking to my daughter, a demon-possessed dope addict girl who has put me through hell for three years.

So I said, "Zona, Honey, come in here and I'll show you. Now, remember, you locked the front door when you came in. See right there; the front door's locked."

She was still shaking, but said, "Yeah, I see it."

Then I showed her that I had locked the back door before I had gone to bed. And she said, "Yes, Daddy. But he didn't use a door, Daddy. I woke up. I woke up, and he was sitting by my bed, just sitting on the floor, looking at me. And — an — and I got so scared, I didn't think I could stand it. He stood up, and he was bigger than the door, and he didn't even bend over. He walked through the door, wall and all!"

"I jumped up out of the bed," Zona continued, "and I went over to the door, then and I watched him, and he walked down the hallway and he didn't even use a door. Daddy, he was so big. When he got here to the kitchen, he just walked through the wall right over the top of the house, and into the air."

"Wow!" I yelled, "God just put meat on one of your angels so you would know you have seen your angel!"

A Chip Off the Old Block

Since the morning Zona's angel appeared to her, she hasn't taken one ounce of dope. She is completely set free! When Bobby heard about it, he began to seek God again too. And God saved him all over again, and delivered him from dope. Then eventually, they got back together, got married again, and started all over. Glory to God forever!

After Zona and Bobby were drug free, born again, and happily married for three years, one day they came to see me, and started telling me they wanted to have a baby.

"Daddy, I think I want a baby," Zona told me.

I couldn't believe my ears.

But there was a problem. When they decided to have a baby, the doctor said they had taken too much dope to conceive.

"You've taken so much dope that you have messed up your body. The anorexia, and the dope together have messed up your insides so badly that you will never be able to conceive.'"

At this point, Zona teared up a little bit, but went on, "The doctor says we might be able to have a baby if I have an operation, but even if I did have the operation, he couldn't promise me that we could. Oh Daddy, I don't want an operation, I just want a baby...." So she just let it drop. I knew if Bobby and Zona were really serious, I would hear more.

Nearly two years had passed when Zona came to my office and said it was still her desire.

"Daddy, I still want a baby, and I was just thinking, you believe that Jesus is a Miracle Worker — could He perform this kind of a miracle for me?"

I said, "Yeah, Zona, He could, but do you really, really want a baby?" After listening to her for a while, she convinced me that she and Bobby did want a baby.

"Daddy, I want you to lay hands on me and ask God to give us a child."

So we went to a pastor who is really successful in praying for barren women. We laid hands on Zona, and agreed in Jesus' name to heal whatever was wrong to make it possible for Zona to have a baby. Then the doctor laid hands on her and prayed that she would conceive. Then we continued to pray and believe, and asked others we had confidence in to pray.

Not long after we got serious with God, Zona got pregnant, and gave birth to a beautiful little girl. I know she is beautiful, because she looks exactly like me. If you're ever in one of my meetings when Zona is there, just see for yourself!

A CHIP OFF THE OLD BLOCK
· · ·

Once when Shambach was helping me in one of my meetings, he walked in and said, "I'm here to see that baby." So he walked over and took one look at the baby and said, "Oh, God! This baby looks like you! Never in my life did I ever see a baby that looked so much like anybody as this baby looks like you!"

Then he said, "Oh, God, please don't let this baby continue to look like Norvel!" (Glory to God.)

"Not two of them on earth! Not two of them!" he went on.

The next couple of times I saw Shambach he told me he was praying for "God to change Zona's baby's looks."

I'm not kidding, she does look like me.

But, glory to God, that's not the end of the story. Not only do Zona and Bobby have a wonderful baby girl, but Zona answered a call from God to minister to women who are overweight or have anorexia. She opened a beautiful exercise place where ladies come to work out and has about thirteen instructors to help her with thirty some classes a week. She also ministers to women and girls who are on drugs.

And she has written her own book called, *Fatness to Fitness*. Zona is no longer a divorced drug addict, covered with knots and boils. She is God's child, totally delivered from the onslaughts of the devil. Blessed be the name of Jesus forever!

It took Zona's guardian angel to "shake her up," and bring about the answer to all the prayers we prayed for her. So never forget, glory to God, that it pleases God to send an angel to set you free from all your bondages.

ANGEL SENDING FAITH
. . .

Angels are real. Oh yeah! Some of them are so much bigger than you can imagine, because it takes a big angel to do warfare, and sometimes they have to do warfare.

> And there was war in heaven: Michael and his angels fought against the dragon; and the dragon fought and his angels,
>
> And prevailed not; neither was their place found any more in heaven.
>
> Revelation 12:7,8

> Yet Michael the archangel, when contending with the devil he disputed about the body of Moses, durst not bring against him a railing accusation, but said, The Lord rebuke thee.
>
> Jude 1:9

And angels can materialize. If you want to know the truth about it, angels can walk through a wall into your dining room and have a meal with you. Then they can get up and walk right back through the wall before your eyes. Angels are created beings. They are ministering spirits. And they will minister to you if God needs them to. If they have to materialize to "shake" someone up, or minister help to someone, God can cause it to happen.

There are also angels that bring us a message or help in other ways:

> And the angel answering said unto him, I am Gabriel, that stand in the presence of God; and am sent to speak unto thee, and to show thee these glad tidings.
>
> Luke 1:19

I know for certain that many of us would be dead today if it had not been for our angel.

Why?

Because this world is full of demons and there is constant warfare in heaven going on between the angels, the demons, and the devil (Jude 1:9).

ACTIVE VOICE OF VICTORY FAITH
GETS GOD IN ON YOUR FIGHT
· · ·

God has armies of angels, and the air is full of demons. So you need to let God in on your fight. You need to get His attention by letting Him know you believe Him in any situation, and that He will deliver you by faith. Anything that comes into your life that is not good, or healthy, or strong, or of good report, is the work of hell.

So if you go to a church and have a pastor who doesn't know anything about binding and casting out demons, and doesn't want to learn about any of it.... Or if you yourself are trying to pastor a church and you don't want to deal with the devil or demons...you might as well be driving a truck! And if you go to a church where the pastor doesn't know anything about binding the devil and dealing with demons, that's crazy.

Why do I say this?

Because devils and demons are here to wreck the human race. If you go to a church where you spend your time and money, and the pastor of the church doesn't know how to deal with the devil, always remember this: You have a choice.

The devil is crazy! He is your enemy, and he's going to do everything he can to get to you. So you had better find some place where they know how to deal with the devil, and love God. Find a church that wins souls for Jesus, throws the devil out, and gets the glory of God in the place.

But you say, "Well, Brother Norvel, they don't have a church like that in my town."

Well then, why don't you pray and ask God for His anointing and guidance? Maybe He will have you build one, or maybe someone else. Glory to God forever. It can be done. And God will visit there, glory to Jesus.

When an angel as big as two men comes down from heaven, he doesn't have to preach a sermon. All he has to do is just appear in a dope addict's room, say, "Look!" And devils look at that big angel, and they go!

When your faith pleases the Lord, He will use you as a faithful servant to minister to others every day. Every day! And He will honor your voice of victory and send angels on your behalf. He will accept your faithful worship and speak to the hearts of businessmen to prosper you financially. He will heal your body, and the bodies of others you pray for. And He will ask you to show others how to walk in God pleasing faith.

That's why I have shared in this book how I learned to follow Him after spending years in a traditional denomination that didn't live in God's world of unseen faith. Glory to God! If He could get my attention, He could get anybody's.

And that's why I have shared how Hulda pleased the Lord in believing, active faith to escape cancer's sentence of death. And how Rock Hudson was born again because of a woman's servant hearted obedience to bring him my tapes. And how my daughter Zona was set free because of active, Bible faith!

If you're following the Lord, you need to know and live in this kind of Bible faith, because, **without faith it is impossible to please him: for he that cometh to God must believe that he is, and that he is a** *rewarder*...get that...*a rewarder* **of them that diligently seek him** (Hebrews 11:6).

Jesus wants you to take care of your body so He can walk in your shoes. Oh yeah! Jesus wants you to stand up like blind Bartimaeus against the unbelief of others and give you a miracle. He wants you to press into the crowd like the woman with the issue of blood so virtue can flow to you. And Jesus wants you to worship Him, like the Canaanite woman, so He can set the captives free.

Pleasing the Lord is easy once you decide to believe God by faith, never doubting that He will always perform His Word. Glory to God! When you obey the Bible by saying and acting on what Jesus said in His Word, He will do anything for you. Because you will be pleasing the Lord. So go do it! Amen.

NORVEL HAYES MINISTRIES

Book, Tapes & Videos

Books

Financial Dominion....................................$10.00

Healing Manual..$10.00

How To Live & Not Die.......................$10.00

Know Your Enemy..................................$10.00

The Ministry For Everyone............$10.00

Understanding The Ministry Of Visions.....$10.00

What Causes Jesus To Work Miracles....$10.00

God's Medicine of Faith.........................$8.00

God's Power Through The Laying On
Of Hands....................................$8.00

Putting Your Angels To Work.................$8.00

Stand In The Gap For Your Children.....$8.00

Training Camp For The Army Of God........$8.00

True Riches [Booklet].............................$2.00

-By Zona Hayes-Morrow

Avenge Me Of My Adversary $8.00

Gossip: Talking your way to hell...........$7.00

Worship God First [Booklet].......................$2.00

Tapes

Prosperity The Bible Way.....................$40.00

How To Deal With Satan &   Demons....$40.00

Secrets To Keeping Your Faith Strong......$40.00

How To Live And Not Die..................$30.00

How To Please The Lord.......................$30.00

How To Pray Effectively.......................$30.00

The Power Of Confession....................$30.00

Becoming A Servant Of God.................$20.00

God's Number One Covenant Worship...$20.00

How To Change Things......................$20.00

How To Make The Devil Leave
You Alone...............................$20.00

What Causes Jesus To Perform Miracles...$20.00

Teaching On Prayer................................$20.00

As Long As I Sought The Lord, He Made Me
To Prosper...............................$15.00

The Fire Of God.............................$15.00

Receiving God's Benefits.................$15.00

Worship The Secret To Finding Favor
With God...................................$15.00

Videos

Don't Give The Devil A Choice..................$20.00

Faith First, Healing Second.....................$20.00

God Honors Specific Faith.......................$20.00

God Works In Atmospheres.....................$20.00

How To Live & Not Die..........................$20.00

How To Pray Effectively..........................$20.00

Laugh At The Devil................................$20.00

My Story: Betty Baxter..........................$20.00

Praying Through......................................$20.00

The Secret Of Success............................$20.00

Victory In Prayer......................................$20.00

Worship The Secret To Finding Favor
With God....................................$20.00

You Must Have God's Attention To
Receive A Miracle............$20.00

You Must Speak To The Mountain....$20.00

Your Healing Is It God's Will?.........$20.00

What Causes The Glory Of The Lord
To Come.................................$20.00

For additional copies or materials, contact:
Norvel Hayes Ministries I P.O. Box 1379
Cleveland, TN 37364-1379 I 423-476-1018
www.nhm.cc

Norvel Hayes shares God's Word boldly and simply, with an enthusiasm that captures the heart of the hearer. He has learned through personal experience that God's Word can be effective in every area of life and that it will work for anyone who will believe it and apply it.

Norvel owns several businesses which function successfully despite the fact that he spends more than half his time away from the office, ministering the Gospel throughout the country. His obedience to God and his willingness to share his faith have taken him to a variety of places. He ministers in churches, seminars, conventions, colleges, prisons — anywhere the Spirit of God leads.

For a complete list of tapes and books
by Norvel Hayes, write:

Norvel Hayes
P. O. Box 1379
Cleveland, TN 37311

*Feel free to include your prayer requests
and comments when you write.*

New Life Bible College

New Life Bible College was founded in 1977 due to a burning desire within me to see God's power set people totally free -to see the crippled walk, sight restored to the blind, the sick healed and the demon-possessed delivered. I have taught the Bible across the nation and overseas in Bible Schools, Full Gospel Businessmen's Conventions, large and small churches, missions, university and high school classrooms, and in federal and state penitentiaries. Satan's power over many lives has been broken and driven out. Many have lived and not died as the Holy Ghost totally revolutionized them, driving out cancers, giving new hearts, straightening crooked limbs, restoring marriages, rescuing souls ...and countless other miracles.

I know the only plan that God has provided for you is VICTORY! This plan is revealed to us through God's word. God's power for victory - the Holy Ghost -performs God's Word, not ideas in the minds of men.

Therefore, to possess the victorious life God has provided, one must begin with sound teaching from the Word of God. At New Life Bible College, the Bible is the only textbook used in the classroom. Our curriculum is designed to lay a foundation of God's Word on the inside of each student so that they can live to the fullest abundant life and take God's mighty power to the world. New Life Bible College is truly a voice to the nations. With the doors constantly being opened in different countries, opportunities are provided to aid and support missionaries and students who have a call to preach overseas. At New Life Bible College we allow the Holy Spirit to minister through the Word to FEED YOUR FAITH and starve your doubts to death.

To request an information packet contact:
New Life Bible College I P.O. Box 1379
Cleveland, TN 37364-1379 I 423-479-7120